W9-CCB-610

The Big Lie

What Every
Baby Boomer
Should Know About
Social Security and Medicare

A selection of other works by A. Haeworth Robertson

The Cost of Social Security: 1975–2050 (1975)

OASDI: Fiscal Basis and Long-Range Cost Projections (1976)

The Outlook for Social Security: 1977–2051 (1977)

Social Security—Prospect for Change (1978)

The Challenge in Long-Range Pension Commitments (1979)

A Commentary on the 1979 Advisory Council Report on Social Security (1980)

The Coming Revolution in Social Security (1981)

The Underlying Problems of Social Security (1982)

The National Commission's Failure to Achieve Real Reform in Social Security (1983)

Social Security's Bleak Future (1984)

Is the Current Social Security Program Financially Feasible in the Long Run? (1985)

The Crisis in the U.S. Medicare System (1986)

What Is in the Future for Public Retirement Systems? (1987)

Financing the U.S. Military Retirement System (1988)

1989 Trustees Report on Social Security's Financial Health: Good News for the Elderly, Bad News for the Young (1989)

Extraordinary Popular Delusions and the Madness of Crowds (1991)

Social Security: What Every Taxpayer Should Know (1992)

Will Anarchy or Socialism Result from Social Security's Future Broken Promises? (1993)

美国的社会保障 (1994 Chinese translation of *Social Security: What Every Taxpayer Should Know,* prepared by Renmin University, Beijing, People's Republic of China)

The Big Lie

What Every
Baby Boomer
Should Know About
Social Security and Medicare

A. Haeworth Robertson

Retirement Policy Institute
Washington, DC

To comment on the book or to order the book in large quantities at a special discount, please address:

Retirement Policy Institute
P.O. Box 53446
Washington, DC 20009

This publication is designed to provide accurate and authoritative information in regard to the subject matter covered. It is sold with the understanding that the publisher is not engaged in rendering legal, accounting, or other professional service. If legal advice or other expert assistance is required, the services of a competent professional person should be sought.

From a Declaration of Principles jointly adopted by a Committee of the American Bar Association and a Committee of Publishers and Associations.

In this book, the masculine pronoun "he" has occasionally been used to refer to both sexes for the sake of simplicity.

Design and composition by Oakland Street Publishing, Arlington, Virginia
Printed by The Mack Printing Group, Easton, Pennsylvania
First Printing: March 1997

Library of Congress Cataloging-in-Publication Data

Robertson, A. Haeworth. 1930–
      The big lie—what every baby boomer should know about social security and medicare.
      xviii, 142 p.: ill.; 21 cm.
      Includes bibliographical references and index.
      1. Social security—United States.   2. Social security—United States—Finance. 3. Medicare. 4. Social problems. I. Title.

HD7125.R62   1997   368.4'3'00973   96-93007
                                          AACR2

ISBN 0-9632345-6-0

Politicians have lied to the American people for too long, pretending we could have everything we wanted. . . . Voters are going to have to demand better, more responsible leadership.

—Senator Warren B. Rudman
The Washington Post, April 21, 1996

The taboos against discussing Social Security and Medicare need to be broken, and broad principles for modifying them need to be proposed. . . . The trouble is that the longer changes are delayed, the more abrupt and unfair they will be. That's why silence is irresponsible. . . . As a moral matter, Americans deserve candor.

—Robert J. Samuelson
The Washington Post, May 15, 1996

Contents

List of Charts

Preface

"**I**'m mad as hell and I'm not going to take it anymore." So went an outburst by the newsman denouncing the hypocrisies of his time in the 1976 movie *Network.*

I now feel the same way about all the lies and hypocrisies surrounding the selling of Social Security to the public during the past 60 years. It was easy to disregard the first half-truth, to overlook an omission here and there, to ignore the first lie, and to give the benefit of the doubt to government officials and policy makers who seemed to be well intentioned but didn't get all the facts straight. But the cumulative effect of twenty years of personal experience with these deceptions is more than I can tolerate any longer. I am compelled to speak out as forcefully as possible about one of the greatest frauds ever perpetrated on the American public.

Not that I've been quiet in the past. When I was brought in from outside the government to be Chief Actuary of the Social Security Administration in 1975 and became aware of the appalling public misunderstanding of Social Security, I immediately began trying to explain what the program really is and how it really works—as distinguished from the program depicted by the propaganda that has been spread shamelessly since 1935. In 1978, I resigned as Chief Actuary so that I would have more time and freedom for this educational effort.

My first full-length book, *The Coming Revolution in Social Security*, published in 1981, warned of all the problems that are now becoming evident. It predicted, among other things, that "the Medicare program as well as the nation's entire health care system will be changed beyond recognition during the next twenty-five years." Now, some fifteen years later, this prediction is rapidly coming true. My next book, *Social Security: What Every Taxpayer Should Know*, published in 1992, reiterated the problems that lie ahead. In addition, I've written more than 100 articles and papers, given more than 500 speeches, and have thus helped explain Social Security to thousands of people. The level of understanding has improved somewhat in recent years, but not nearly enough.

I'm reminded of the cartoon during the energy crisis in the early 1970s. A woman is sitting in her gas-guzzling sedan with the engine running, and the filling-station attendant is holding the hose pouring gas into the car. After a few minutes, the attendant says, in desperation, "Lady, would you please turn the engine off, you're gaining on me." As Social Security's problems mount, and as the public becomes more disenchanted with it, a giant propaganda machine turns out more and more lies to lull the public into a false sense of security that is destroying their will and ability to create their own financially sound retirement.

This book represents one last personal attempt to dispel the myths that have grown up about Social Security and to wake up the public to the perils that lie ahead if the program is not revised to meet our needs appropriately at a price we can afford to pay. I say this is my "last attempt" not because I'm growing weary but because if we do not take action by the year 2000, it will be too late. Frankly, it is already too late to make a smooth transition to a new system (we should have acted in the early 1980s). A very bumpy transition can be made in the late 1990s. But after the year 2000, we will be trapped: It will then be obvious to everyone that the present Social Security program won't work and that its continuation will result in massive social and economic turmoil, yet it will be too late to implement a revised program without causing a different form of social and economic turmoil that is equally disturbing.

My prior "outreach efforts" have been honest and direct yet somewhat moderate compared to this book, in which I have continued to be honest and direct but no longer gentle. Gentleness and mildness have not been effective enough in the past to cause the public and the policymakers to focus attention on the gigantic Social Security problems that lie ahead—problems that are much more serious and have broader consequences than most people realize.

At the urging of colleagues I have included two of my earlier essays about Social Security—one stating the need for actuaries, as well as others, to stand up and be counted (Appendix C), and the other stating the unfortunate and unintended consequences of not doing so (Appendix D). Since this book is such an uncompromising challenge to the prevailing myths about Social Security, I (and you) should expect a hostile, outraged reaction from those who have perpetuated those myths. I say, only, let the facts speak for themselves.

Washington, DC   A. Haeworth Robertson
January 1997

Basis for Social Security Benefit Provisions and Financial Projections

The Social Security benefit provisions contained in this book are those in effect on January 1, 1996. These benefit provisions form the basis for the 1996 Annual Reports of the Boards of Trustees of the Old-Age and Survivors Insurance, Disability Insurance, Hospital Insurance, and Supplementary Medical Insurance Trust Funds, that were submitted to Congress on June 5, 1996. For more details on the operation of the Social Security program (including Medicare), reference should be made to these reports or to subsequent Trustees Reports that are usually issued in April of each year.

Sometimes the terminology used to describe Social Security can be confusing. Social Security includes several benefits or programs:

- Old-Age, Survivors, and Disability Insurance benefits (OASDI)
- Medicare-Hospital Insurance benefits (HI)
- Medicare-Supplementary Medical Insurance benefits (SMI)

Social Security "payroll taxes" are used to finance the OASDI and HI programs. SMI is financed mostly by general revenue paid by all taxpayers, and partly by "premiums" paid by participants who are over age 65.

Throughout the book, the term Social Security usually refers to all of the above programs (OASDI, HI, and SMI), unless otherwise noted or suggested by the context.

The Big Lie

What Every
Baby Boomer
Should Know About
Social Security and Medicare

1

The Gross Deception of the Public

It is true that you may fool all the people some of the time; you can even fool some of the people all the time; but you can't fool all of the people all the time.

— *Abraham Lincoln*

You have never been told the whole truth about Social Security, by any administration. More bluntly put, you are an unwitting victim of The Big Lie.

"Interesting times lie ahead. The public is beginning to catch on to the inter-generational transfer nature of Social Security." These words of a top-level official slipped out in 1974 as I was being interviewed for the job of Chief Actuary of Social Security. This was my first inkling that the public is on its own in trying to figure out exactly what Social Security is and how it works. Indeed, the principle of *caveat emptor* applies just as much to the purchaser of Social Security as it does to the purchaser of a used car—and the stakes are much larger.

In 1975, six months after I accepted the job of Chief Actuary, a book that was very critical of Social Security was published by an investigative reporter. Standard operating procedure was to assign a team of experts, drawn from different areas of the Social Security Administration, to critique such attacks. The emphasis was always on what was wrong with the attack, not on what was right with it. There was plenty wrong with this particular book since it was not written by someone who really understood social insurance. Nevertheless, it contained many valid points. During our review session, the team member from the public information office, referring to the book's inaccuracies and misleading statements, said: "Why did he have to say all of that? The truth would have been bad enough!"

In 1976 I began an education campaign within the Social Security Administration to explain how Social Security really works. I explained, for example, that an individual's contributions (taxes) are not saved and invested for his future retirement but the taxes of one working generation are used to pay for the benefits of a different, retired generation; that an individual's benefits are virtually unrelated to his past taxes; and so on. In the middle of one of these educational sessions, a career employee exclaimed, "But that's not how we were taught to explain Social Security to the public."

In 1978, because of all my work in trying to improve the public's understanding of Social Security, I was asked to lead a session on "Public Misunderstanding of Social Security." This was at a weekend retreat for the top ten Social Security offi-

cials. Following my presentation, everyone agreed
that public understanding of Social Security was
abysmally low and that real trouble lay ahead if this
misunderstanding continued—particularly in view
of the inevitable tax increases and benefit cuts for
the baby boomers and their children. Faced with
this problem, what should we do? One top official
summed it up this way: "All of the myths and mis-
understandings about Social Security are sort of a
religion for the public. We can't take that religion
away without substituting something. What would
we substitute?" It seemed to me that we should simply tell the truth about how Social Security works
and let the chips fall where they may. No one else at
the meeting agreed or, at least, was willing to say so
in front of his peers.

A few weeks after that experience, which was a
culmination of many similar disturbing events during my three years as Chief Actuary at Social
Security, I left government service so that I would
have more time and freedom to speak out about
how Social Security really works.

Now, some twenty years later, are you being presented any clearer picture of Social Security? Yes, to
some extent, but for every obfuscation that has
been cleared up, a new one has arisen. For example, you are now being sold the myth that your
excess Social Security taxes are being "saved" to
help meet the high future cost of retirement benefits for the baby boomers.

Furthermore, the Social Security Administration
is still trying to shield its employees, as well as the
public, from the truth about Social Security. I was

recently invited by the supervisor of a midwestern branch office of the Social Security Administration to speak to his employees at a weekly meeting to which outside speakers were regularly invited. I sent advance material I had written explaining the latest Trustees Reports so that we could have a more fruitful discussion about how the system works and about its projected long-term financial problems. Three days prior to the meeting the supervisor telephoned to say that "the powers that be do not really want you to speak to us," adding that he didn't want to jeopardize his chances for an upcoming promotion. The "powers that be" turned out to be his district manager and his area manager.

Who is responsible for this gross deception of the public? Why would anyone want to misrepresent a program that many consider to be one of the most successful social experiments in U.S. history? This deception is not the result of an organized conspiracy; rather, it has arisen and been perpetuated by an unfortunate combination of factors: arrogance, ignorance, and self-preservation.

Arrogance

Some people have the paternalistic, arrogant attitude that they know what is best for you and that whatever is necessary to achieve *their* goals for what *they* perceive to be best for you is justified. If they have to misrepresent the facts or hide future costs, that is okay in order to minimize public discontent and keep those Social Security taxes rolling in. Right now, the first priority of this group is to restore public confidence in Social Security, even though such confidence cannot be justified in the long term for the present set of benefits. To achieve this goal, they are trying to keep discussion of Social Security's weaknesses to a minimum and they continue to claim that today's benefit promises can be fulfilled. Anyone who is relying on these promises for a secure retirement in the 21st century is in for a rude awakening.

First Lady Hillary Rodham Clinton portrayed the essence of such arrogance when she was being questioned in 1994 about her health care reform scheme. She said, in exasperation at all the questioning about the future cost of her proposal:[1]

> When Franklin Roosevelt proposed Social Security, he didn't go out selling it with actuarial tables. . . . He basically said, "Look, here's the deal: you pay; you're taken care of; you have social security in your old age."

That may have been the way things were done in the past; however, the public is not quite so naive and trusting these days.

Ignorance

Some people just don't know any better. The government has misled the public over the past 60 years about many important aspects of Social Security, as will be pointed out later. When the arrogant and the ignorant have disseminated false information in the past, the media has frequently accepted the information at face value without checking its accuracy—after all, there are tight deadlines to meet and the subject is complicated. This, in turn, has compounded public misunderstanding. The public, never having had Social Security explained to them thoroughly and correctly, is understandably confused and thus plays an important role in the further spreading of misinformation.

Self-Preservation

Politicians want to get reelected every few years so they can continue to "serve the public." Who can blame them? But, because of the misunderstanding created by the arrogant and the ignorant, politicians cannot tell the truth about Social Security and get reelected. Some of them have learned this the hard way. There is good reason why Social Security is referred to as "the third rail of American politics—touch it and you're dead." In addition to this impediment to revealing the truth, as if it were not enough, some politicians fall into the category of the arrogant or ignorant, at least in the area of Social Security.

People who played a role in conceiving, designing, and expanding Social Security—particularly in the 1930s and 1940s—naturally believe they did the right thing. They believe that if it should have been done a different way, they would have done it that way. They view anyone who suggests that a system designed in a past era may not be appropriate for tomorrow as irresponsible and a panicmonger.

Many employees at the Social Security Administration and the Health Care Financing Administration (which administers the Medicare part of Social Security) have the mistaken notion that their job is to defend and maintain Social Security's status quo (or, in some cases, to expand Social Security); whereas their real job is to administer—and explain accurately—the system as it exists at any given time. This mistaken notion is what prevented the Social Security supervisor mentioned above from exposing his employees to an outside speaker and thus risking the loss of a promotion. Unfortunately, these attitudes are all too prevalent throughout the Social Security Administration and the Health Care Financing Administration. They are obviously not in the best long-range interest of the public.

The public itself is partly responsible for its own deception about Social Security. George Bernard Shaw explained this phenomenon best when he said, "A government which robs Peter to pay Paul can always depend on the support of Paul." The past and present generations of benefit recipients have had a strong self-interest in not asking too many questions about how Social Security could pay such generous benefits from such meager taxes.

The baby-boom generation, which does not expect to receive these windfall benefits, is more forthcoming with questions about why they will probably receive such meager benefits from such generous taxes. And for the children of the baby boomers—sometimes called Generation X—the disparity between taxes paid and benefits received will be even greater. This highlights the obvious fact that the "public" is made up of many different groups, each with its own special interests. And it illustrates the potential conflicts inherent in our present Social Security system which, in the words of former Senator Russell Long, "is nothing more than a promise to a group of people that their children will be taxed for that group's benefit."

Finally, there are several organizations—and a few individuals—that have built their membership and funding base and power on the principle that Social Security should not be revised, unless it is to expand the already unsustainable benefits. It would be difficult for such organizations to maintain this posture if the whole truth were known about Social Security.

The Need for the Truth—Now

In this day and age, it is more difficult than in the past to deceive the public, at least for very long. Even if continued deception were possible, it is, of course, totally inappropriate. Let's tell the public the truth about Social Security. If the public likes the truth, they will have confidence in the program and they will support it, financially and otherwise. If the public doesn't like the truth about Social Security—as seems more likely, based on the growing public discontent—Congress can revise the program so that the majority of the public will believe it to be fair and reasonable and thus pay the taxes necessary to support it.

Sounds simple and reasonable, doesn't it? Of course, when the public fully understands the truth about Social Security, the result might be a disturbing turmoil until the program is revised to suit a majority of the public's expectations of fairness and appropriateness. And this would be harmful to those mentioned earlier who are perpetuating all the myths about Social Security. On the other hand, if we persist in keeping the public in the dark, it is true that the turmoil will be delayed but it is also true that the turmoil will be greater once it does occur—perhaps so great as to be unmanageable.

Justice John Paul Stevens made the following comments about "keeping people in the dark" in a 1996 Supreme Court opinion:[2]

> Bans against truthful, nonmisleading commercial speech . . . usually rest solely on the offensive assumption that the public will respond "irrationally" to the truth. The First Amendment directs us to be especially skeptical of regulations that seek to keep people in the dark for what the government perceives to be their own good.

In view of the government's dismal record in accurately describing Social Security to the public, it is ironic that Congress passed a law, effective April 1, 1995, that provides stronger penalties for "individuals or groups who purposefully mislead the public about Social Security or Medicare services." This was duly reported in the *Social Security Courier*, January 1995, which went on to state that if you believe you have received misleading information, you may report it to:

Social Security Administration
Office of Public Affairs
Misleading Advertising
P.O. Box 17740
Baltimore, MD 21235

You may want to keep this address in mind for those times when you hear public statements about Social Security, including Medicare, that don't agree with the facts.

Do you remember the Medicare Catastrophic Health Plan passed by Congress in 1988? It was repealed just one year later in 1989 when the public found out enough details to decide they didn't like it. In the end, the people—and not the politicians—really do have the final say about Social Security.[3] All we have to do is get informed and let our views be known. When that happens, politicians, instead of being defeated for discussing Social Security's deficiencies, will be defeated if they do *not* discuss the need for Social Security reform.

2

Myth #1
Your Contributions Are Used
to Provide Your Benefits

> *In general, the art of government consists of taking as much money as possible from one class of citizens to give to the other.*
>
> *—Voltaire*

The benefits you receive have very little, if anything, to do with the Social Security taxes that you and your employer pay. The myth that your contributions are used later to provide your benefits is at the root of all our attempts to understand Social Security's problems and to resolve them.

During the first 40 years or so after Social Security was adopted, the government tried to convince you that your taxes were used to provide your benefits—that you got what you paid for.

This was done in a subtle way by borrowing terminology from the insurance and banking institutions and using such terminology (inappropriately) to describe Social Security. The rhetoric went something like this:

> Social Security is an "insurance" program
> under which you have an individual "account"
> and you and your employer pay "contribu-
> tions" into a "trust fund" and thereby build up
> an "earned right" to receive benefits when you
> become ill or disabled, die, or retire.

After 40 years of this rhetoric, repeated in one form or another, people began to believe that they were buying and paying for their own benefits. This misunderstanding was crucial to the acceptance of Social Security in its early years, for two reasons.

First, from the standpoint of the beneficiary: In the 1940s many people would not accept pensions that they considered to be a dole or a handout from the government. And it was obvious in the early years that this was exactly what Social Security was. So, propaganda was concocted to convince people that they had an "earned right" to these benefits because of their "contributions," thus making the program morally acceptable.

Second, from the standpoint of the taxpayers: It was much more palatable to make "contributions" to a national "insurance" program under which "earned rights" to pension benefits were being built up than it was to pay taxes for a welfare program.

In this regard, consider the following comments made by President Franklin D. Roosevelt, respond-ing to a visitor who complained about the economic effect of the Social Security tax:

> I guess you're right on the economics, but those
> taxes were never a problem of economics. They
> are politics all the way through. We put those

> payroll contributions there so as to give the
> contributors a legal, moral, and political right
> to collect their pensions. . . . With those taxes
> in there, no damn politician can ever scrap my
> social security program.[1]

Beginning in the mid-1970s, the public began to
understand that they were really paying taxes, not
so-called "contributions." They learned that the so-
called "trust funds" had no economic substance
and that there wasn't any money in their so-called
"accounts." They learned that their so-called "insurance" was social insurance, which is not the kind of
insurance where benefits are commensurate with
the premiums paid by an individual, or even by a
group of individuals. In other words, they began to
understand that their taxes bore virtually no relationship to their benefits. And finally, in the past
few years, they learned that they didn't have an
"earned right" to anything as Congress effectively
cut retirement benefits for some 23 percent[2] of the
retired population by taxing such benefits, elimi-
nated students' benefits even though the deceased
parent had satisfied all conditions for their payment, reneged on promised inflation protection,
increased the normal retirement age for persons
born after 1937, and so on.

Of course, it is still not widely understood and
accepted that there is virtually no relationship
between taxes paid and benefits received. When a
proposal is made to reduce the cost-of-living adjustment for retirees, the immediate response is, "You
can't do that; I've bought and paid for my own benefits with 40 years of tax payments." When a retired

person learns that his Social Security benefits may be reduced if he continues to work, his immediate reaction is, "That's not fair; I've paid my taxes and bought my benefits; you can't take them away from me now."

When trying to figure out whether Social Security is a "good deal" or a "fair program," most laymen—and a surprising number of experts—insist on comparing an individual's taxes with his benefits. They try to figure out the "return" on an individual's "investment." I cannot emphasize too strongly that this is a futile exercise because Social Security (with its benefit structure and its pay-as-you-go financing method) was never intended to provide individuals with benefits equivalent to their "contributions"; therefore, it does not. Furthermore, Social Security was never intended to provide a particular generation with aggregate benefits that are equivalent to their aggregate "contributions"; therefore, it does not.

In recent years, and in response to all the questions asked by the public about the relationship between taxes paid and benefits received, the Social Security actuaries have made several studies, unpublished as well as published. In addition, I have made studies on my own.

One such study[3] concluded that some workers should pay a Social Security tax of 4 percent of their earnings (with a limit on taxable earnings) and other workers should pay 29 percent (matched, in each case, by equal employer taxes) in order for total taxes to be equivalent to total benefits during the lifetime of the worker and his or her dependents. By way of contrast, the actual tax rate (in

1996) was 6.2 percent for a worker, matched by equal employer taxes. This study took into account only the old-age, survivors, and disability benefits and taxes, and it excluded Medicare.

For the Hospital Insurance part of Medicare, the discrepancy between taxes paid and benefits received is even more striking. Social Security taxes to finance Hospital Insurance benefits are currently 1.45 percent of a worker's salary, with no limit on taxable salary (matched by an equal employer tax). Currently (in 1996), a worker earning $20,000 per year pays $290 per year in Medicare taxes; an executive with a salary of $1,000,000 per year pays $14,500 per year in Medicare taxes; yet both receive the same Hospital Insurance benefits. Incidentally, if you move to another country upon retirement, no Medicare benefits will be paid (even though you may have thought you bought and paid for such benefits during your working years).

Furthermore, the taxes paid by a particular generation of workers are not necessarily equivalent to the cost of the benefits that generation will eventually receive. An actuarial study[4] as of January 1, 1990, of the entire Social Security program, including Medicare, concluded that during the first 50 years of Social Security's existence, the total taxes paid by employees and employers combined had amounted to only one-half of the value of the benefits that had been paid or promised with respect to this period of participation. In other words, during the past 50 years, if the Social Security tax rates had been twice what they were, they would have been adequate to pay for the benefits that were "earned"

during that period. The result of this past generosi-
ty is, of course, an unfunded accrued liability (as of
1990) of $12 trillion: the amount by which benefits,
paid or promised with respect to earlier years of participation in the system, exceed the amount of taxes
paid during those years by employees and their
employers (appropriately adjusted for assumed
interest earnings).[5]

Thus, as of January 1, 1990, the nation had a "hid-
den liability" of approximately $78,000 for every
adult between ages 20 and 65, or more than $46,000
for every living man, woman, and child, regardless
of age. This was four times the national debt of $3
trillion as of January 1, 1990, the government's offi-
cially acknowledged liability.

Miss Ida May Fuller of Ludlow, Vermont, the program's very first recipient of a monthly pension, provides a simple example of how an individual does
not get what he or she pays for, and how a liability
can be passed on to future generations to pay. Miss
Fuller paid only $22.00 in Social Security taxes prior
to her retirement but lived to collect $20,884.52 in
retirement benefits.

Obviously, this $20,862.52 discrepancy must be
paid by someone other than Miss Fuller. What in
fact happened is the $20,862.52 was "borrowed"
from Social Security taxes paid by other taxpayers
and, in effect, forms part of the $12 trillion unfunded
accrued liability that must be paid eventually by
future taxpayers.

Individuals do not evaluate welfare programs
(such as Supplemental Security Income or Aid to
Families with Dependent Children) on the basis of

whether the individual taxpayer receives benefits that are equivalent to his taxes. In evaluating our public school system, an individual does not insist that his family receive direct benefits equivalent to his school taxes. (People who use parochial or private schools receive no immediate, direct benefit from taxes used to support public schools.) Similarly, with respect to the national defense effort and the highway system and the public libraries, the individual does not examine the relationship between his taxes and his direct benefits.

Why, then, is there this preoccupation with comparing individual taxes with individual benefits under the Social Security system? It is simply that Social Security has been misrepresented and misunderstood for so long that most people still firmly believe that Social Security is something that it is not and something that it was never intended to be.

This misrepresentation is still going on and is still endorsed by important officials. As recently as January 1995 during a conference in Washington, D.C., sponsored by the National Academy of Social Insurance on the future role of Social Security, the question of "income redistribution" was being discussed. Of course, the more income redistribution, the looser the connection between what an individual pays in contributions and receives in benefits. The luncheon speaker, then a high-ranking government economist who was a founder and former president of the Academy, stated from the podium that we "should be less explicit in explaining the degree of income redistribution in Social Security if we are interested in low-income persons . . . too much clarity is not a good idea...the redistribution element in Social Security should not be transparent." These statements are particularly ironic since the avowed goal of the Academy is "increasing public understanding of social insurance programs."

This same government official went on to say that "Social Security is a covenant between generations that can be sustained only if Social Security has political immunity." This suggests that if the public truly understood Social Security, they would insist that it be changed in ways not approved of by the luncheon speaker.

The speaker's idea of a "covenant between generations" is interesting in view of former Senator Russell Long's observation that "Social Security is nothing more than a promise to a group of people that their children will be taxed for that group's benefit." Is it responsible to have a covenant (particularly an "unfair" covenant) between a generation of workers and their children, many of whom are yet unborn? Thomas Jefferson did not seem to think so when he wrote:

> We may consider each generation as a separate nation, with a right, by the will of the majority, to bind themselves, but not to bind the succeeding generation, any more than the inhabitants of another country.

Neither did Thomas Paine believe that such covenants were appropriate when he wrote:

> Every age and generation must be as free to act for itself in all cases as the ages and generations which preceded it. The vanity of gov-

erning beyond the grave is the most ridiculous and insolent of all tyrannies.

During the first 40 years of Social Security's existence, the public was pleased with the program because it misunderstood the way Social Security worked. The people paid low taxes, received high benefits, and yet were led to believe they were paying their own way. In time, however, this same misunderstanding has led the public to build up expectations about Social Security that can never be realized because of the way it is designed and financed. And this same misunderstanding is making it extremely difficult to recognize and acknowledge the problems that lie ahead and to make the changes in the Social Security system necessary to make it viable for today's young workers. The nation is paying a large price for all these past years of blissful misunderstanding.

3

Myth #2
Your Benefits Are Guaranteed
by the Government

After reviewing the evidence, the Council is unanimously convinced that all current and future Social Security beneficiaries can count on receiving all the benefits to which they are entitled.

—1979 Advisory Council Report on Social Security

This hypocritical statement was boldly presented on page one of the final report of the 1979 Advisory Council on Social Security on December 7, 1979. Later in this same report, with contemptuous disregard for their previous statement that beneficiaries could "count on receiving all the benefits to which they are entitled," the Advisory Council made the following statements:

- A majority of the Council recommends that half of the Social Security benefits be included in taxable income for federal income taxes.

- A narrow majority of the Council urges that serious consideration be given to enactment now of an increase in the normal retirement age under Social Security that would be effective at about the turn of the century.

Both of these recommendations were clearly for reductions in benefits, albeit in a roundabout way. (And both of them were adopted in 1983.)

In still other sections of this same report, the Advisory Council seemed to acknowledge that additional benefit reductions would be necessary early in the 21st century. References were made to:

- reducing the growth of scheduled benefits.
- benefit reductions as a means for achieving financial balance in the system.
- reduction in the rate of growth of real benefits.
- the fact that if these projections are borne out, Social Security revenues would have to be increased or benefits would have to be cut.

It is not with 20/20 hindsight that I challenge the veracity and consistency of the Advisory Council's statements of reassurance. Soon after these audacious statements were issued, I pointed out their inappropriateness:

- on January 21, 1980, in a guest appearance on the nationally televised *MacNeil-Lehrer Report* entitled "Social Security: Facing the Cost";
- in February 1980, in testimony before the Senate Finance Committee's Subcommittee on Social Security; and
- in March 1980, in testimony before the President's Commission on Pension Policy.

The basic assignment of the Advisory Council was

to identify problems in the Social Security system and to propose solutions. In issuing its statement of reassurance that all promised benefits would be paid, the Advisory Council appears to have been desperately trying to achieve another goal: to arrest the public's growing fears about whether Social Security is going to be able to make good on its promises.

It should be noted that there are two kinds of promise associated with Social Security: promises about the benefits that will be paid and promises about the taxes that will be collected to pay for those benefits. What has the record been since 1979 on Social Security's promises about benefits and taxes?

In 1983, Social Security was amended to reduce benefits and increase taxes in the following important ways:

- Cost-of-living adjustments were deferred for six months, from June to December 1983.
- The normal retirement age was increased by two years, from age 65 to age 67, for persons born in 1960 and later. For persons born between 1938 and 1959 the normal retirement age was increased by smaller amounts.
- Beginning in 1984, part of Social Security's monthly cash benefits (but not more than 50 percent) became subject to federal income tax for persons with high incomes in retirement ($25,000 if single and $32,000 if married). This was an effective benefit reduction, since benefits were formerly tax exempt.
- Social Security tax-rate increases originally

scheduled for 1985 and 1990 were advanced to 1984 and 1988, respectively.

In 1994, 85 percent (instead of 50 percent) of Social Security's monthly cash benefits became subject to federal income tax for persons with high incomes in retirement.

Medicare benefits are currently being reduced, a development that began in the 1980s. This is being achieved by various means, including limitations on amounts reimbursed to hospitals and physicians.

What can we expect during the next 25 years regarding Social Security benefits and taxes? Here is a summary of the most likely changes if the entire system is not otherwise reformed.

- Higher Social Security payroll taxes; and increased use of nonpayroll taxes (such as general revenue or a value-added tax) to finance Social Security as taxpayers resist further increases in the more obvious payroll tax.
- A normal retirement age of 70 or higher for persons born after 1960; and smaller increases in the normal retirement age for persons born earlier.
- Increased taxation of Social Security benefits, resulting in an effective reduction in those benefits.
- Decreased cost-of-living adjustments in pensions, particularly for those at the upper end of the benefit scale.
- Decreased Medicare benefits, particularly for higher income retirees; and taxation of the imputed value of Medicare benefits. Also, there will be increased rationing of medical-care services.

During the first forty years of Social Security's history, there was a steady expansion of both the type and level of benefits provided and the percentage of workers required to participate. The Social Security Act was passed in 1935. Survivors benefits were added in 1939. Disability benefits were added in 1956. Medicare benefits for beneficiaries aged 65 and older were added in 1965. Medicare benefits for disabled beneficiaries, regardless of age, were added in 1972. The benefit for an average wage earner increased from about 30 percent of his pre-retirement earnings in 1950 to some 43 percent at the present time. Social Security applied to about 60 percent of all working persons in 1937; today it applies to 96 percent. Medicare-Hospital Insurance payroll taxes are now paid by 98 percent of all workers.

In discussing the social programs of the Great Society, President Lyndon B. Johnson once said that we should not ask what a new program will cost, but how good it will be. In the heady 1960s almost anything seemed possible.

But, inevitably, economic realities caught up with us in the 1970s, and we began to realize that it was, indeed, possible to think up more programs than we could finance. Try it in your own life: Make a list of all the things you would like to have or do in order to be content. Do you have enough money to achieve this? Probably not. Similarly, on a collective basis, the nation does not now produce enough to satisfy a "wish list" of everything that everyone needs or deserves or wants in order to be content.

The nature of the "government guarantee" of Social Security benefits is not well understood. A private employer who, in a formal pension plan, has promised specified benefits because of prior service cannot reduce those benefits without incurring severe penalties imposed by laws adopted by Congress. In private pension plans, "vesting" is also an important concept and is required by law. By way of contrast, the government is above the law, so to speak, and the public has no legal claim to continuing Social Security benefits. In theory, at least, the entire Social Security program could be terminated by Congress at any time. Section 1104 of the Social Security Act provides that "The right to alter, amend, or repeal any provision of this Act is hereby reserved to the Congress." As a practical matter, it is reasonable to assume that Social Security will continue without abrupt change; but it is not reasonable to assume that all of the benefits currently being promised will, in fact, be paid. This is demonstrated by a review of the promises that have been renounced, as noted above, during the past fifteen years.

The fact that the government has renounced Social Security benefits in the past and that it will do so in the future does not mean the government is nefariously plotting to cheat or disappoint the public. It does mean, however, that the government has used bad judgment in making long-term commitments. Furthermore, it seems likely that at least some elected officials realized they were enacting benefit promises that were more generous than could be fulfilled, but they made the promises anyway just to please current voters.

Consider the nature of "government promises," "government-sponsored" programs, "governmental responsibility," and having the "government *pay*" for things. Sometimes we behave as if the "government" not only *should* be ready to help us in time of financial need, but that the "government" *owes* us something—a retirement benefit, support for our dependents if we die, and so forth. When something in our lives goes wrong, the first place many people look for help is to the government. Who is this "government" we keep looking to for help? Where does it get its money? We all know the answer: The government is simply a system we have established and a group of people we have hired or elected to carry out our wishes. Bureaucrats and politicians do not have any money to give us except what we ourselves have paid in taxes. When we demand a benefit from the government, we are demanding it from our friends and neighbors.

It cannot be emphasized strongly enough that casual references to "governmental responsibility" or having the "government pay" for all or part of Social Security are extremely misleading. Stripped to its essentials, a governmental program like Social Security is just an agreement among the people of the nation that one segment of the population will receive certain benefits and that another segment of the population will pay for such benefits (with a certain amount of overlapping). The government may administer and enforce compliance with a program, but, in the final analysis, any governmental program is paid for by and is for the benefit of the people of the nation. The government is simply the intermediary that carries out the wishes of the people.

Accordingly, it is up to us to prevent the government from making future commitments that our children and grandchildren cannot keep. It is up to us to elect officials who will seek out expert advice, and heed it, to ensure that tomorrow's workers can afford the taxes necessary to pay for the Social Security promises that we are making today. Your Social Security benefits are not guaranteed by the government. They are guaranteed by future taxpayers, who may or may not be willing and able to honor that guarantee.

4

Myth #3
A Trust Fund Is Being
Accumulated to Help Pay
Retirement Benefits to the
Baby Boomers

The emperor, stark naked, walked in the procession under his crimson canopy. All the people in the town declared that the emperor's clothes were beautiful. None of them was willing to admit that he hadn't seen a thing; for if anyone did, he would be considered either stupid or unfit for his job.

"But the Emperor has nothing on at all!" cried a little child.

—*"The Emperor's New Clothes,"*
by Hans Christian Andersen

We are being told that Social Security is accumulating huge trust funds that will help pay retirement benefits to the baby boomers. However, the trust funds are stark naked; there is nothing in them that can be used to pay future benefits. There are only treasury bonds, which are merely promises that the government will collect additional general revenue from the public in the future.

Here are some of the words and phrases used by the government to describe this alleged trust-fund buildup. "Special trust funds are set aside to pay future benefits." "Some money is put in reserves." Most of the payroll taxes are used to pay current benefits, "the rest is invested." As recently as August 1995 (in SSA Publication No. 05-10080), the government stated that the excess of income over outgo is "invested in U.S. Treasury Bonds, the safest of all possible investments. Those reserves will accumulate, earn interest and be used to help pay for the retirement of the baby boom generation beginning around 2010." On December 22, 1994 in a letter to *The Washington Times*, Dr. Shirley S. Chater, the Commissioner of the Social Security Administration stated:

> Social Security is building large reserves and making investments to help finance benefit payments to the aging baby boom generation.

At best, this is a gross misrepresentation of how the excess Social Security taxes are used. It would be more forthright, however, to call it part of The Big Lie.[1]

This lie is being told over and over in a vain attempt to restore public confidence in Social Security's ability to make good on its exorbitant future promises. The fact that public confidence is declining is dramatically revealed by a 1994 survey of the young, sponsored by the Third Millennium,[2] indicating that more of them believe in Unidentified Flying

Objects than believe that Social Security will honor its current benefit promises to them.

The truth is, the trust funds do not have assets or investments of the type that represent savings that will help pay future benefits. Because of the manner in which Social Security has created and invested trust funds, Social Security will simply pass on to future generations the liability for benefits currently being earned. Here, in effect, is a summary of how the trust funds work:

• Social Security taxes are collected from employees and employers and deposited in trust funds.

• Benefits are paid from the trust funds, and any money not required for current benefit payments is loaned to the federal government, which promptly spends the money for other purposes and issues interest-bearing bonds to the trust funds.

• The government pays interest on the bonds by issuing still more bonds to the trust funds.

• In future years when then-current Social Security taxes are inadequate to pay benefits, the bonds will be paid off, or redeemed, and the proceeds will be used to make benefit payments.

The $64,000 Question is how will the government get the money to pay off the bonds when they are needed to pay Social Security benefits? The answer is simple: the government will collect general revenue from taxpayers at the time the bonds are redeemed (unless the government borrows the necessary funds and thus passes the liability on to yet another unsuspecting generation of taxpayers).

In other words, when the government tells us

that it is collecting extra Social Security taxes and building up a trust fund to make it easier to pay for future retirement benefits, what it is really doing is borrowing money from current Social Security taxpayers to meet current government expenses, and promising to repay the amount borrowed (with interest) by collecting additional taxes (general revenue) from future taxpayers.[3]

Here's another way to think of this question of setting aside money to pay future retirement benefits. Assume that you are a family of four: you and your spouse and two children. You decide to save part of your current earnings for retirement. You deposit the savings with a trustee that has these two choices as to their investment:

1. Buy stocks and bonds and real estate that can be sold when you retire.
2. Immediately spend the savings and put an IOU in your safe-deposit box—an IOU promising that your savings plus interest will be repaid by your children from their future earnings when you retire.

Which investment option makes you feel more secure? Option 1, of course, where your savings are invested, not spent.

If the Social Security trust funds were invested in stocks and bonds and real estate we could legitimately say the "reserves had been set aside to pay future benefits." However, this is not permitted under current law. Accordingly, the trust funds are loaned to the government and immediately spent, with the promise that the loans will be paid by our children's future taxes. Of course, our children did not sign these IOUs (treasury bonds); they are probably not aware that they have this liability; and they may not be willing or able to repay the IOUs when they come due.

Perpetrators of this trust fund myth will try to confuse you with such statements as, "treasury bonds are as good as gold" or "the United States government has never defaulted on a treasury bond yet." These gratuitous observations completely miss the point: namely, that the existence of treasury bonds in the Social Security trust funds does not reduce the total future tax collections (from payroll tax and general revenue combined) necessary to pay future benefits. Neither does the existence of treasury bonds in the trust funds represent "reserve funds set aside to pay future benefits."

This trust fund myth will be hard to dispel. Supporters of the status quo will use every trick they know to perpetuate this myth, but a careful analysis of the facts speaks for itself. So long as the trust funds are loaned to the government and spent (rather than truly invested outside the government), it is both meaningless and misleading to claim that the trust funds are "making investments to help finance benefit payments to the aging baby boom generation."

5

Myth #4
The Present Social Security Program Is Affordable and Can Be Financed by Modest Changes in Benefits and Taxes

Let me make clear what [the President's] position is. We will save Medicare. We will stop efforts to hurt Medicare and will do it within a balanced budget plan.

—Vice President Al Gore
Vice-Presidential Debate
October 9, 1996

This is perhaps the biggest lie of all. It is certainly the most harmful, and it is the lie that is leading us slowly but surely down the path of social and economic collapse.

Of course, this lie takes many forms: "If you elect me, I won't touch your Social Security." "We shall protect the Social Security trust funds and prevent the government from using them for other purposes." "The Social Security system is financially sound until well into the next century."

On June 6, 1996, the Trustees Reports were released indicating that Medicare is in dire financial straits, with benefits projected to far exceed tax income. The Secretary of Health and Human Services was asked at a news conference whether retirees might be facing fewer services or higher costs under Medicare. She replied, "Absolutely not." This is a typical knee-jerk political response: Never admit that there is a problem.

What is the truth about the outlook for Social Security, including Medicare? Can it possibly survive the onslaught of baby boomer retirements without major change? The answer is NO.

To consider this question, let us think of the retirement benefits provided by Social Security in this way: A person who retires at 65 receives monthly benefits under the Social Security program, made up of two parts:

- A cash annuity, payable monthly for life, adjusted explicitly to reflect increases in the Consumer Price Index (CPI).
- A medical care annuity, payable monthly for life, which increases implicitly as the cost of medical care increases.

The medical care annuity is not paid in cash, of course; it is paid in kind, in the form of medical care insurance protection under the Hospital Insurance (HI) and Supplementary Medical Insurance (SMI) programs. Taken together, these two programs are called Medicare.

The approximate monthly value of this insurance protection for HI and SMI benefits can be determined from the annual Trustees Reports. Here are some examples of average monthly medical care annuities compared with average monthly cash annuities being provided in 1995.

	Retired Worker over Age 65	*Retired Worker and Spouse over Age 65*
Cash Annuity	$ 705	$1,215
Medical Care Annuity		
–HI	265	530
–SMI	146	292
	$411	$822
Total	$1,116	$2,037

For the retired worker alone, the medical care annuity of $411 is 58 percent of the cash annuity of $705. For the retired worker and spouse, the medical care annuity of $822 is 68 percent of the cash annuity of $1,215.[1]

Medicare benefits are clearly an important part of a person's retirement benefits. For years it was common practice to say that Medicare was part of Social Security. In fact, government agencies bragged about how Social Security provided medical care benefits as well as cash benefits. Then in the late 1970s the financial outlook for both parts of Social Security began to look bleak. The government did very little to fix the long-term Medicare problems, but it did take steps to alleviate the long-term cash benefits financial problems. In order for public officials to make reassuring statements about the financial health of "Social Security," it was necessary to exclude Medicare from the term "Social Security program." This practice has generally been followed ever since by government agencies and many analysts and commentators.

It is now possible, therefore, for the government to reduce Medicare benefits, which represent nearly 40 percent of the value of total retirement benefits paid, and for politicians to say, "I didn't touch your Social Security benefits." This change in the definition of Social Security was an ingenious way to misrepresent the financial condition of Social Security—and, indeed, your prospects for a financially secure retirement—without actually telling a lie.

In order to measure the financial soundness of Social Security, each year the Trustees Reports present a comparison of projected income and outgo for the next 75 years—the maximum remaining lifetime of someone just entering the work force. The purpose, of course, is to see if income and outgo are in balance. If they are not, then benefits or taxes, or both, should be adjusted.

These projections must be based upon assumptions about future economic conditions, birth rates and mortality rates, etc. Since there is no way to know exactly what the future holds, the Trustees select three different sets of assumptions that span a range considered reasonable by most professional analysts. These assumptions are used to produce low-cost, intermediate-cost, and high-cost projections. The intermediate-cost projections are used by the government for planning purposes and for all pronouncements on the financial health of Social

Security. My personal opinion is that the actual future cost will be closer to the high-cost projections.[2] Moreover, if the benefits provided by Social Security are to be considered firm promises (as most retired people seem to assume they are), the so-called high-cost projections should be used to determine whether future income and outgo are in balance and the promises can be kept.

Appendix A compares projected income and outgo under all three sets of assumptions for the different parts of Social Security: the monthly cash benefits (old-age, survivors, and disability benefits); and the Medicare benefits (Hospital Insurance and Supplementary Medical Insurance).

Chart 5.1 in this chapter shows a more limited comparison of income and outgo. Projections are based on the 1996 Trustees Reports under the intermediate assumptions during the fifty-year period from 2010 to 2060. This period approximately covers the retired lifetimes of the baby boomers who will reach age 65 some time between the years 2011 and 2029; this is obviously the period of time in which baby boomers should be interested. The projected income for the SMI program reflects the premium income from the participants based upon current law, under which the participants pay a steadily declining portion of the total cost; it does not include income from general revenue.

Chart 5.2 is the same as Chart 5.1 except that it is based on the so-called high-cost assumptions.

One look at Charts 5.1 and 5.2 makes it clear that grossly inadequate provision has been made to collect the taxes necessary to provide the benefits

Chart 5.1

**Comparison of Projected Expenditures and Income,
During the Period 2010-2060, for Each Part of Social Security,
Based on Intermediate Assumptions**

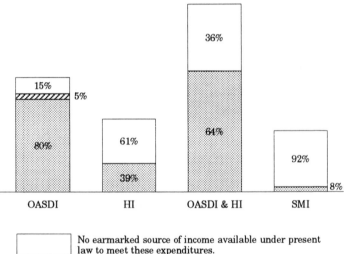

| OASDI | HI | OASDI & HI | SMI |

No earmarked source of income available under present law to meet these expenditures.

Expenditures met by liquidation of trust funds, and interest on trust funds.

Expenditures met by earmarked income (payroll taxes, income taxes on OASDI benefits, and SMI premiums).

that have been promised the baby boomers. Of course, this means that major decreases in benefits or increases in taxes must be made. For example, according to Chart 5.2 (based on high-cost projections), if income and outgo are to be brought into

Chart 5.2

**Comparison of Projected Expenditures and Income,
During the Period 2010-2060, for Each Part of Social Security,
Based on High Cost Assumptions**

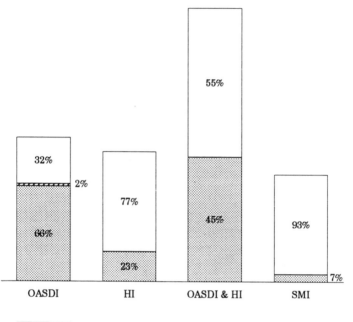

No earmarked source of income available under present law to meet these expenditures.

Expenditures met by liquidation of trust funds, and interest on trust funds.

Expenditures met by earmarked income (payroll taxes, income taxes on OASDI benefits, and SMI premiums).

balance during the period 2010–2060: OASDI benefits must be reduced by 32 percent or taxes must be increased by 48 percent, on average during the period; HI benefits must be reduced by 77 percent or taxes must be increased by 335 percent. Even under the intermediate projections shown in Chart 5.1, substantial decreases in benefits or increases in taxes must be made to bring income and outgo into balance.

If we examine the projected cost and projected tax income for the period 2010 to 2060, for the OASDI and HI programs combined, we find that provision has been made to collect only 45 percent of what is needed to pay benefits under the high-cost projections; and only 64 percent under the intermediate projections.[3]

Regarding the SMI program, the law states, in effect, that general revenue will be collected in whatever amounts are necessary to provide the part of the cost not paid by participant premiums. Yet, no provision has been made in a long-range budget to meet this open-ended and extremely high-cost commitment. Under present law the portion of the cost paid by participant premiums will continue to decrease; and during the period 2010–2060, it will amount to only 7 percent of the total cost under the high-cost projections, and 8 percent under the intermediate projections.

Finally, the charts make it clear that the highly touted trust fund buildup that is supposed "to help pay retirement benefits for the baby boomers" is just a figment of some demagogue's imagination. If the trust fund buildup under the OASDI program is used to cover the deficits under the HI program, there will be nothing left in any of the trust funds by the year 2010 to help pay for the baby boomers' retirement. Even if the trust fund buildup is preserved to pay OASDI benefits during the baby boomers' retirement years, it will cover only 2 percent of the cost under the high-cost projections and 5 percent under the intermediate projections.

And remember, as pointed out in Chapter 4, when they say the trust fund's treasury bonds will be used to pay benefits, they really mean that additional—but unscheduled—general revenue must be collected in order to redeem those bonds.

If you belong to the baby boom generation, or to Generation X, the next time a politician tells you that your Social Security benefits are safe and secure, tell him to start looking for another job because you are going to vote for someone who will tell you the truth. Anyone who will misrepresent a program that is vital to your future personal financial well-being will probably misrepresent everything else.

6

Myth #5
You Can Expect to Retire in
Your Early Sixties

*Given three requisites—means of existence,
reasonable health, and an absorbing interest—those years beyond sixty can be the
happiest and most satisfying of a lifetime.*

—*Earnest Elmo Calkins*

If you are under age 50, it is unrealistic to expect
to retire in your early 60s. Your early 70s is more
like it. There are lots of reasons this is true.

First, as you saw in Chapter 5, without major tax
increases the benefits under the Social Security system will have to be reduced for persons retiring
after about 2010. The most obvious way to do this
(for reasons noted later) is to increase the retirement age.

In fact, even though many people don't realize it,
the 1983 Social Security amendments already provide for a normal retirement age later than 65 for

persons born after 1937 and who, therefore, reach age 65 after the year 2002. An individual's normal retirement age (the age at which full benefits are paid without actuarial reduction) now depends upon his year of birth, as shown in the following table. The normal retirement age applies not only to the primary beneficiary but also to a spouse who may be eligible for benefits. (For widows, the normal retirement age schedule is slightly lower for persons born before 1962.)

Year of Birth	Normal Retirement Age
1937 or earlier	65
1938	65 years, 2 months
1939	65 years, 4 months
1940	65 years, 6 months
1941	65 years, 8 months
1942	65 years, 10 months
1943–54	66
1955	66 years, 2 months
1956	66 years, 4 months
1957	66 years, 6 months
1958	66 years, 8 months
1959	66 years, 10 months
1960 or later	67

Further increases in the normal retirement age to at least age 70 seem likely for persons born after 1945.

This is not bad news; rather, it is a natural consequence of living longer and being in better health at higher ages. Chart 6.1 compares the remaining life expectancy for persons aged 65 in 1940 (when Social Security benefits were first paid), in 1995, and in 2050 (about the time when the children of

Chart 6.1

**Remaining Life Expectancy for Persons
Reaching Age 65 in Selected Calendar Years**

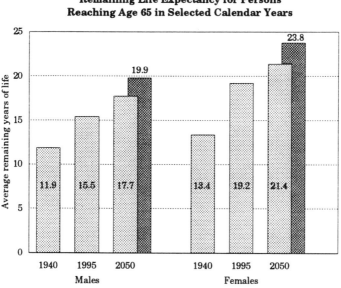

Note: Two projections are shown for 2050, based on the "intermediate" and "high cost" assumptions, respectively.

Source: *1996 Annual Report of the Board of Trustees of the Federal Old-
Age and Survivors Insurance and Disability Insurance Trust
Funds.*

the baby boomers will be reaching 65). For retirees
in the mid-21st century: males will be living another
18 to 20 years after reaching age 65, instead of the
12 years in 1940; females will be living another 21 to
24 years, instead of the 13 years in 1940. These are
astounding changes.

Furthermore, when the baby boomers reach age
70, males will have a remaining life expectancy of
12 to 13 years (more than the remaining life
expectancy of 11.9 years for a 65-year-old male in
1940). Females at age 70 will live another 16 to 17

years (more than the 13.4 years for a 65-year-old female in 1940). For males and females combined, retirement at age 65 in 1940 is approximately equivalent to retirement at age 74 for the baby boom generation, if we think in terms of the remaining life expectancy after retirement.

Chart 6.2 is a graphic illustration of why the average retirement age will increase. It compares the size of the working population that pays Social Security taxes with the size of the beneficiary population that receives Social Security benefits. The size of these two segments of the population is shown at three points in time: 1950, 1995, and 2030. The figures for 2030 are estimates based upon the low-, intermediate-, and high-cost sets of birth rate and mortality assumptions.

A quick look at Chart 6.2 will indicate how the tax burden on the working population has grown and will continue to grow. The obvious way to reduce this burden is to redefine "old age" and thus simultaneously increase the size of the working population and decrease the size of the beneficiary population.

The idea that one should retire at age 60 or 65 (or that one is "entitled" to retire then) is a relatively new idea. In 1950, 76 percent of the male population between ages 60 and 64 was actively employed. In 1995, only 53 percent of this same age group was working. For males between ages 65 and 69, the percentage working declined from 57 percent to 26 percent between 1950 and 1995. If we were able to work until our late 60s in 1950, we should be able to do it in the 21st century when health and working conditions will be more favorable.

Chart 6.2

Past, Present, and Projected Covered Workers, Retired Workers, and Other Social Security Beneficiaries

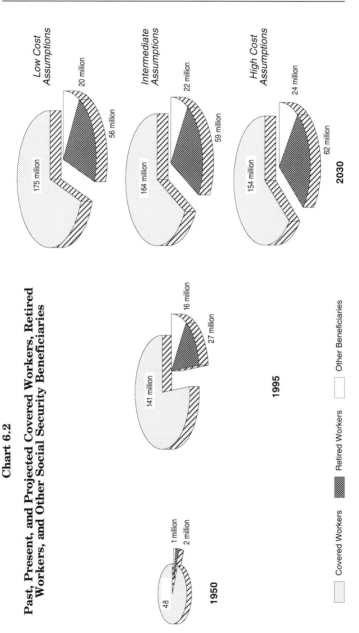

Low Cost Assumptions

20 million

56 million

175 million

Intermediate Assumptions

22 million

59 million

164 million

High Cost Assumptions

24 million

62 million

154 million

2030

16 million

27 million

141 million

1995

1 million

2 million

48

1950

Covered Workers   Retired Workers   Other Beneficiaries

Apart from the role a higher retirement age would play in alleviating Social Security's financing problems, the customary retirement age is bound to increase for a more important and fundamental reason. If people keep retiring in their early 60s, the resulting work force will not be large enough to produce all the goods and services needed by the entire population.

Until recent years, retirement was generally an all-or-nothing situation; that is, it was customary to work full-time until retirement and then not at all. A recent trend has been to partially retire, and to continue in part-time paid employment in one job or another. This trend will continue as a natural consequence of the following factors: the need for older employees in the work force as the growth in the labor force slows because of the lower birth rates since the mid-1960s; the need for retired workers to supplement their pensions as inflation and taxation continue to erode their purchasing power; and the sense of self-worth and the feeling of belonging that part-time employment can provide for older workers. Full-time retirement does not always provide the rewards and satisfactions needed for a contented life.

Related to this trend toward part-time employment will be more flexibility in the age when full-time employment ceases. This will be compatible with a fuller implementation of age-discrimination-in-employment laws, two-wage-earner families, job-sharing arrangements, and a general work environment that is more accommodating to individual preference.

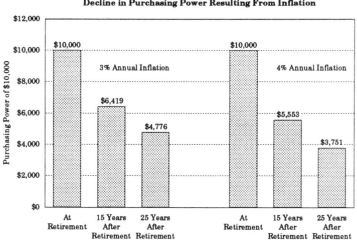

Chart 6.3
Decline in Purchasing Power Resulting From Inflation

A few words about inflation and its effect on the retirement age may be in order. We used to think inflation of 3 or 4 percent was unacceptable. After the extremely high inflation of the 1970s and early 1980s, inflation of 3 or 4 percent per year may seem mild. However, it can have a devastating effect on a fixed retirement income. Inflation of only 3 percent per year will reduce the purchasing power of a $10,000 pension to $6,419 in 15 years and to $4,776 in 25 years. Inflation of 4 percent per year will reduce it to $5,553 in 15 years and to $3,751 in 25 years. This is graphically illustrated in Chart 6.3. Higher inflation—not completely out of the question—would absolutely destroy the purchasing power of a pension in just a few years. Inflation, or the threat of inflation, will force most people to work—at least part-time—well into their 70s, if health permits. Although Social Security pensions are adjusted automatically for cost-of-living changes (at the present time), most other pensions are not.

As Loren Dunton, President and Founder of the National Center for Financial Education, puts it: "Hard work, saving and investment, and a little luck will enable some people to retire in their early 60s or even sooner. But for the average person born after 1945, it is more realistic to assume that full retirement will not occur until age 70 or later."

7

Myth #6
Social Security Cannot Be
Abolished or Changed
Drastically

*If we are going to accomplish anything in
our time we must approach our problem in
the knowledge that there is nothing rigid or
immutable in human affairs. History is a
story of growth, decay and change. If no
provision, no allowance is made for change
by peaceful means, it will come anyway—
and with violence.*

—Herbert Hoover

The protectors of the present Social Security system tell us that the system is so large and complex and that it has been in existence so long that it
is virtually impossible to make substantial revisions
at this time. Wait a while longer, they say, there will
be plenty of time to make changes in the years
ahead "if change really proves to be necessary."
   In a disingenuous statement to the U.S. Senate

Special Committee on Aging, presented on September 24, 1996, Robert J. Myers—the 84-year-old, erstwhile Chief Actuary of the Social Security Administration—said:

> It is not a certainty that there is a long-range financing problem. The low-cost estimate shows that none is present.

Having thus put his audience at ease by minimizing the seriousness of the financial crisis when baby boomers begin to retire, he admits later in his statement that "it is only prudent to take some reform action soon, although the changes could well be deferred to take effect some years in the future, as well as being instituted gradually."

It is perfectly clear that major problems lie ahead. There is no need to wait and see. The basic numbers of people who will receive benefits and who will pay taxes can be determined today with reasonable certainty; and it is the ratio of taxpayers to beneficiaries at any given time that is one of the most important determinants of Social Security's cost. Consider the following.

All of the people who are going to receive old-age retirement benefits at any time during the next 50 years are alive today. Of the total Social Security taxes that will be paid during the next 50 years, 85 percent will be paid by people who are now alive. For the first 25 years the figure is 99 percent. Any reasonable projection based on people who are alive today will demonstrate conclusively that future benefit outgo will far exceed tax income (as discussed in detail in Chapter 5). Changes will certainly have to be made to close this gap between income and outgo; and the longer the changes are postponed, the more drastic the changes and the greater the disruption.

The next time you are advised by a politician or an advocacy group that there is no need to take action now about a problem that they admit "may" occur 15 or 20 years in the future, just remember the following story.

> You and your friends are in a party boat floating down a lazy river in a beautiful national park. A retired park ranger, who has studied the course of this river for years, shouts a warning from the shore that there is a gigantic waterfall ahead and you should pull over to the shore and revise your plans for the rest of the trip.
>
> How can this be true, you ask. Your government-provided map of the river does not indicate a waterfall anywhere near this area. It would be easy at this point to pull to shore, but this very ease makes it appear less necessary—so you continue on.
>
> The river grows rougher and more people appear on the shore, shouting warnings of what lies ahead. Finally, as you near the waterfall, its sound and fury are almost drowned out by the hordes of people on the shore shouting their warnings. By then, however, it is too late to save everyone on the boat. Only by throwing the weaker people overboard will the boat be maneuverable enough to reach the shore. Otherwise, everyone will go over the waterfall to their destruction.

A few of us began to give warnings of Social Security's future problems in the mid-1970s.[1] By 1981, with the publication of *The Coming Revolution in Social Security*, I was shouting. During the past three years, more and more people have begun to sound alarms. According to a survey conducted in mid-1996 by Washington Counsel, P.C., a Washington-based law firm, over thirty organizations were currently undertaking, or planning to conduct, studies about Social Security reform.

We are nearing the Social Security waterfall, and unless we take action soon, here is what lies ahead during the first two decades of the 21st century—which begins in less than four years.

Bitter conflict between the baby-boom generation, who want their promised benefits, and their children, who will not be able to pay the exorbitant taxes required to finance such benefits. Drastic benefit cuts. Severe tax increases. Strikes and demonstrations. Angry baby boomers, unexpectedly having to work into their 70s, well past their planned retirement dates. Continued erosion in the credibility of the government that made these unrealistic promises and waited so long to admit its error in judgment. Political elections won and lost because of divisive demagoguery. Reduced standard of living resulting from a total national output of goods and services inadequate to satisfy public desires—because of a work force that is too small, too disgruntled, and too highly taxed. A generally disillusioned public: disdainful of government, disappointed with the past, and with no hope for a better future.

Social Security involves long-range promises. Planning for retirement is a long-range project. When problems are foreseen, they must be resolved years in advance. Last-minute fixes don't work.

Ironically, the "protectors" of Social Security—who glibly say not to worry now about problems that won't arise until the future—are in reality its "destroyers." By not encouraging solutions to the system's imminent problems, in the 1980s and 1990s when they were still manageable, these protectors have *guaranteed* that there will be severe social and economic disruption during the years from 2000 to 2020 as the inevitable reforms of Social Security are made. And have no doubt about it, significant changes must and will be made.

8

A Time for Action

I want you to get mad, to go to your window and open it, and stick your head out and yell: I'm mad as hell and I'm not going to take it anymore!

—*A call to action by a disenchanted TV news reporter, Howard Beale, in the 1976 movie* **Network**

Howard Beale was an angry prophet denouncing the hypocrisies of his time. He was particularly frustrated with the actions of his TV network employer, which went to outrageous lengths to raise its viewer ratings based on the theory that the end justified the means.

Following this same theory for the past 60 years, the founders and perpetuators and defenders of the Social Security system have engaged in an unconscionable publicity campaign to sell the system to the American public, even if it required misrepresentations, half-truths, and outright lies.

The public has a right to know exactly how Social Security works; that it will cost more in the future than tomorrow's taxpayers will be willing and able to pay; that the trust funds do not represent "savings" that can be used to pay future benefits; that the steady erosion in benefits that began in 1977 will continue in the future; and that if major changes are not made very soon in Social Security, the resulting conflict and turmoil between the baby boom generation and their children will leave an awful mark on society for the next 100 years.

So, if you adopt the battle cry, "I'm mad as hell and I'm not going to take it anymore," and insist on full disclosure of the truth about Social Security, what's the next step? Exactly what should you do? First, insist that the politicians—starting with your own elected officials—tell you the truth about Social Security. Here is a summary statement of that truth. (Most of these items were discussed in more detail in earlier chapters.)

Benefits and Taxes

The system is not designed to pay benefits to an individual that can be provided by his own taxes. In other words, an individual should not expect to receive his money's worth from his taxes—at least measured by personal benefits received. Instead, Social Security was designed to be a complex system of income redistribution: for example, from later generations to earlier generations; from high-wage earners to low-wage earners; from single workers to married workers with children. Individuals pay Social Security taxes that are a fixed percentage of their income but receive benefits that are related to their presumed need. On average, persons retiring during the past 60 years have received much more in benefits than their taxes (together with their employers' taxes) could provide. Eventually, someone has to pay for this largesse; therefore, persons retiring during the next 60 years should expect to receive less in benefits than their taxes can provide.

Financing Method

Social Security is financed on a pay-as-you-go basis with no advance accumulation of funds to pay benefits due in the future. In other words, current workers pay taxes that are used to pay benefits to retired workers and other beneficiaries. This is in contrast to advance funding methods used under most employer-sponsored pension plans, or when an individual saves for his own retirement. When Social Security collects more than enough to pay benefits in a given year, the excess is spent by the government. The government then promises to repay these amounts in the future by collecting taxes from future taxpayers. The government does not "save" or "invest" these excess Social Security taxes to use for future benefit payments.

Financial Condition

Current Social Security tax income is adequate to pay current benefits, except under the Medicare-Hospital Insurance program. Based on projections made by the Social Security Trustees, however, outgo will soon begin to exceed tax income under each part of the Social Security program: in the year 2003 for Disability Insurance and 2014 for Old-Age and Survivors Insurance, based on the intermediate projections; or, based on the high-cost projections, in the year 1999 for Disability Insurance and 2000 for Old-Age and Survivors Insurance. Under the Hospital Insurance program, outgo began to exceed tax income in 1992, and today the "trust funds" are already being liquidated in order to pay benefits.[1]

This deficit is not a temporary phenomenon; it will continue and will grow rapidly for the foreseeable future. Therefore, drastic changes must be made in all parts of Social Security between now and the year 2020: first for Medicare benefits and then for the cash benefits (old age, survivors, and disability benefits). Benefits must be reduced or taxes must be increased. Even when the "trust funds" are used to pay benefits, an increase in taxes (general revenue) will be required to redeem the treasury bonds in order to pay benefits (unless the government borrows the money to redeem the bonds and thus postpones the eventual collection of taxes needed to pay off the bonds).

Retirement Age

Currently, most Americans retire in their early 60s. Persons born after 1945, however, should expect to retire in their early 70s, although they might work only part-time in their later years. A later retirement age will reduce many of Social Security's financial problems; however, this is not the principal reason for increasing the retirement age. The primary reason for this later retirement age is to maintain (approximately) the present ratio of workers to non-working adults, and thus to have a large enough work force to produce sufficient goods and services for the entire population.

Eligibility for Medicare benefits, now age 65, will probably be postponed to match the new, higher normal retirement ages under Social Security (unless Medicare is absorbed in a new national health insurance plan covering everyone, regardless of age).

Medicare Benefits

Medicare is out of control, and major reforms must be enacted. Continued debate about *whether* changes should be made is ridiculous. The only justifiable debate is about what kinds of changes should be made.

The average cost of medical care has increased nearly twice as fast as the general cost of living since Medicare was adopted in 1965—a predictable consequence of providing generous medical care benefits but making someone other than the recipient responsible for paying the bill. The Hospital Insurance part of Medicare is financed by a tax of 2.90 percent of payroll shared equally by employee and employer. By the mid-21st century when all the baby boomers will have retired, this combined tax would have to rise to 10 percent of payroll under the intermediate projections and 20 percent of payroll under the high-cost projections.

The long-range cost of the Supplementary Medical Insurance part of Medicare is seldom mentioned; however, its cost (expressed as a percentage of HI payroll for ready comparison) is projected to rise, by the mid-21st century, from 2 percent in 1995 to 8 percent under the intermediate projections, and 15 percent under the high-cost projections. The total Medicare program could thus cost as much as 18 to 35 percent of payroll by the time the children of the baby boom generation begin to retire. Moreover, Medicare pays for only about 45 percent of the total medical expenses of persons over age 65.[2]

The above costs refer only to those eligible for Medicare—generally those aged 65 and older. Of additional concern is the cost of medical care for active workers and their families; Medicaid for those on welfare; and some 35 million people— mostly women and children—not covered by any form of health insurance, not even Medicare.

The present half-hearted efforts at medical care reform are nothing compared to the frenzied efforts that lie ahead. During the coming months and years, we will be debating national health insurance, the moral and ethical questions of rationing medical care, euthanasia, federal control of hospital costs and physicians' salaries, government-provided vouchers with which to buy health insurance, payment by beneficiaries of a larger share of the cost of health insurance, forcing hospitals to close and consolidate, luring more retirees into HMOs and managed-care plans, and a host of related issues. As unpleasant as these debates may be, continued neglect and denial of this looming medical care problem would be even worse.

What is the Answer?

It will not be easy to get your politicians to tell you the above truths, for two reasons. First, many politicians have not yet admitted these truths, having fallen victim to all the past lies and misrepresentations about Social Security, including Medicare. Second, even if they know these truths, they won't dare admit them to you because you will vote them out of office—and they will have to find other jobs.

So what is the answer to this dilemma? The answer starts with *you*. You should insist that politicians tell you the truth and you must be willing to accept the truth. If they don't know the truth, you should tell them the facts, as outlined above. And if they will not acknowledge the facts, you should vote for someone who will. Appendix B contains the names and addresses of selected national officials, together with samples of letters you might want to send them.

Maybe your friends will say, "But if we make the politicians admit the truth, they will change Social Security and other institutions in such a way that it will harm us personally. Benefits may be cut; taxes may be increased. Maybe we're better off with the status quo."

The status quo is not a choice that is available to us. No matter what you say or do, no matter what the politicians say or do, we are rushing down a river with a dangerous waterfall ahead. The only decision for us to make is this: Do we want a relatively easy rescue now, or do we want a frantic, disorganized and futile rescue at the last minute?

Once the need for Social Security reform is admitted, the hard part begins: designing a revised Social Security system that is understood and perceived as fair and reasonable by the majority of the citizens, and that results in an appropriately sized, healthy work force that can produce all the goods and services the citizens need and want. Chapter 9 presents a specific proposal for such a revised system of Social Security.

9

The Freedom Plan

There is no doubt that the real destroyer of the liberties of any people is he who spreads among them bounties, donations, and largesse.

— *Plutarch*

As noted in Chapter 5, there will be an ever-widening gap between Social Security income and outgo in the years ahead. In simple terms, the gap must be closed by increasing taxes or decreasing benefits. There is no other choice.

However, there are many different ways in which benefits can be decreased and/or taxes increased; that is, there are many different solutions. Each solution is based on an underlying philosophy about the extent to which an individual should have freedom of choice and thus be responsible for himself; and the extent to which an individual's activities should be regulated and dictated by the government, with the consequent decrease in self-responsibility and increase in reliance upon others. Moreover, any solution must acknowledge the broader challenge of yielding a work force of suitable size and qualifications, and a level of national savings, required to produce all the goods and services to satisfy our needs—particularly in view of our maturing population.

Once you force the politicians to acknowledge the need for change in the Social Security system, you can expect a long and heated debate over exactly what changes ought to be made. This is as it should be in our large, diverse nation.

Proposed changes in the Social Security system are already starting to emerge from the various think tanks, advisory councils, and a few daring members of Congress. This chapter presents for your consideration an outline of the Freedom Plan, a comprehensive revision of our present Social Security system. Naturally, it reflects my own ideas about what kind of Social Security system will produce a healthy and prosperous society. And it is based on some necessary compromises as we make the difficult transition from a system with countless outstanding promises and trillions of dollars of liabilities.

Transition Provisions

Millions of people are receiving retirement and Medicare benefits now or will receive them within a few years. It seems clear that we should continue these benefits without change, if at all possible. Social Security promises are long-range promises, and any changes should be made, if at all, slowly over a long period to give individuals ample time to adjust their financial plans. Here is one possible set of transition provisions.

Continue to make the same benefit payments for the entire Social Security program (Old-Age, Survivors, and Disability Insurance; Hospital Insurance; and Supplementary Medical Insurance) without major change through December 31, 1999. Continue the same total tax payments; however, make reallocations of taxes from the OASI program to the HI program as necessary to pay benefits. On January 1, 2000, there will be a small trust fund balance in the OASI and DI programs and a small or zero balance in the HI program.

Comment: During this period, revisions should continue to be made in the Medicare program (both HI and SMI) to control costs yet keep medical care at an acceptable level. This could be part of a major overhaul of the nation's entire medical care system. Relatively minor changes may be appropriate in the DI program, in accordance with studies already under way.

Individuals aged 55 or older on January 1, 2000 and others receiving benefits on that date (retirees, disabled persons, survivors of deceased workers, etc.) will continue to participate in the entire Social Security program in effect on January 1, 2000, without change, for the balance of their lifetimes.

Comment: It must be noted, however, that in the years ahead many changes will be made in the HI and SMI programs, as well as in the nation's entire medical care system. The principal guarantee with respect to persons at or near retirement should relate only to the amount they pay for HI and SMI benefits. For example, a retired person who paid

HI taxes throughout his working lifetime, in exchange for promised HI benefits during retirement, should not now have to pay additional amounts for HI benefits.

Future Social Security taxes (including those allocated to Medicare) paid with respect to these individuals who continue to participate in the present Social Security program, together with the existing trust fund balances, will not be adequate to finance their future benefits. The government should recognize this deficit or unfunded accrued liability, an estimated $14 trillion[1] as of January 1, 2000, by issuing treasury bonds to the trust funds. This lump-sum amount of $14 trillion in treasury bonds plus the existing trust fund balances, together with interest thereon, and future Social Security taxes paid by these individuals and their employers, will be sufficient to pay all their future benefits.

It is important to note that the issue by the government of $14 trillion in treasury bonds does not represent the creation of new debt; rather, it is simply the formal acknowledgment of debt that already exists but has not heretofore been formally acknowledged. It is this "hidden debt" that has kept the public from fully understanding the gigantic financial obligations being built up under Social Security and passed on to future generations. It should also be noted that putting $14 trillion of treasury bonds in the trust funds does not mean that benefits are fully funded; it is simply a formal acknowledgment that the government must collect additional taxes (or borrow additional amounts) in order to redeem these treasury bonds and make good the system's benefit promises.

Comment: These treasury bonds will, of course, have to be paid off, or "redeemed," gradually over the years in order to make benefit payments. The options available to the government to redeem these bonds will be discussed more fully after the concept of Freedom Bonds has been introduced in the next section.

It may be easier to comprehend an amount like $14 trillion when it is compared with some other large amounts. For example, in mid-1996 the formally acknowledged federal debt was $5.2 trillion. In the year 2000, it is estimated that the Gross Domestic Product (the total output of goods and services by the entire nation) will be about $9 trillion.

Freedom Plan

Individuals who are less than age 55 on January 1, 2000, have paid Social Security (including Medicare) taxes or contributions during their whole working lifetime as required by law. They expect to continue paying such taxes at approximately today's levels. Naturally, they expect to receive future benefits approximately equal to those provided by the current law. The problem is that this is impossible. Either future taxes must be increased or future benefits must be decreased—and by substantial amounts.

Furthermore, there is no clear understanding for most participants about what future benefits are supposed to be and what relationship such benefits have to an individual's taxes. Many people still believe their benefits should be approximately those that can be provided by their taxes.[2] When told this is untrue, they believe they have been cheated or treated unfairly. This poses a whole set of problems that defy solution. Yet, one way or another the problems must be resolved. One possible solution is outlined in the remainder of this chapter.

Persons less than age 55 on January 1, 2000, will no longer participate in the present Social Security and Medicare programs. They will not pay taxes to them and they will not receive benefits from them. Each such person will receive Freedom Bonds (issued by the U.S. Treasury) equal to the individual's past contributions, including the employer's matching contributions, for Social Security and Medicare (excluding the portion of such contributions that was used to provide Survivors Insurance benefits and Disability Insurance benefits), together with interest on such net contributions at the rate payable each year in the past on 30-year treasury bonds. The Freedom Bonds will be placed in the individual's Freedom Account, which will increase each year with interest at the rate then payable on 30-year treasury bonds. (During the period from 1960 through 1995 this interest rate fluctuated from a low of 3.7 percent in 1960 to a high of 13.3 percent in 1981. In 1995 it was 6.9 percent.) The treasury bond interest rate is, in effect, a "real" interest rate, plus some recognition of inflation.

Comment: The government has recently decided to issue Inflation-Linked Treasury Bonds, which are expected to yield a return of about 3.0 to 3.5 percent plus the rate of inflation. These bonds, with suitable modification, could be used as Freedom Bonds.

Under the present Social Security system, an individual's benefits are defined in terms of average wages, length of par-

ticipation, family status, etc., and not primarily on the basis of his Social Security taxes or contributions. Benefits that had "accrued" on this basis as of January 1, 2000, would be replaced by benefits defined in terms of the size of the Freedom Account—which consists initially of the part of the individual's actual past contributions that have not been used to provide disability and survivors benefits (including similar employer contributions made on his behalf), together with interest earnings.

In some cases the value of this newly defined benefit will be lower than the old benefit; in some cases it will be higher. In the aggregate, the value of the new benefits will be lower than the old benefits. However, the new benefits will be defined in such a way that it will be more difficult to reduce them (or make an error in their payment) without the participant's knowledge than it would have been to reduce the old benefits—which certainly would have been cut.³ Also, the new benefits will be "fair." Each individual will get what he pays for—which is the way many people think the current system works.

In making this initial issue of Freedom Bonds, the intent is to "refund" the part of the past Social Security and Medicare contributions (by both the employee and the employer) that has not been used to provide benefits to the individual; namely, the contributions for Old-Age and Hospital Insurance benefits. No refund is made of the part of the individual's contributions allocated to the Survivors Insurance and Disability Insurance programs, since the individual has received "term insurance" protection against these contingencies. On average, approximately 75 percent of past employee and employer contributions, plus interest, would thus be "refunded" in the form of Freedom Bonds.⁴

This newly defined benefit will result in the issue of approximately $7 trillion in Freedom Bonds. This may appear to be an increase of $7 trillion in the national debt, but it is not. It is simply a formal acknowledgment of a government debt to these taxpayers that is a small fraction of the amount owed them under the old Social Security system for benefits they accrued with respect to their past service (but which was not formally acknowledged).[5] In other words, the Freedom Plan will not create any new debt; it will simply substitute one type of formally acknowledged debt for another type of unacknowledged debt that was going to have to be partially renounced.

Beginning January 1, 2000, all participants in the Freedom Plan will make contributions to the system equal to 7.65 percent of their covered earnings. This will be matched by employer contributions. In other words, the same taxes, or contributions, will be paid under the Freedom Plan as under the old Social Security system. There is an important difference, however. All of the Freedom Plan contributions will be used to buy Freedom Bonds, which will be added to the other Freedom Bonds in the individual's account. Furthermore, each individual will have the option to select investments other than Freedom Bonds for up to 50 percent of the total new contributions made to his account after January 1, 2000. Such investments could be in stocks, bonds, real estate, various mutual funds, etc. Each individual could thus gain more and more control over the investment of his Freedom Account as it continues to grow.

This Freedom Account would be the basic fund that each individual would use to provide benefits for himself and his family in the event of retirement, disability, illness, or death. It could be viewed as an IRA, medical savings account, and 401(k) plan, all rolled up into one account.

Comment: The Freedom Account would be advance funded to the extent that investments are made in stocks and bonds and real estate, etc., and not in Freedom Bonds. To the extent that contributions are invested in Freedom Bonds, they would be available for the government to borrow in order to make benefit payments.

Eventually, as much as half of each individual's Freedom Account could be invested in stocks and bonds and real estate, etc., with the remainder in Freedom Bonds—according to the individual's choice. Even more control over the investment decisions could be given to the individual. Provision could be made for an individual to discontinue personal contributions to the Freedom Account, once the account balance exceeded some minimum size that would ensure a certain minimum retirement income. Any additional savings could thus be invested entirely at the individual's discretion, apart from the Freedom Plan. Also, an individual could eventually be given the choice of investing more than half of the Freedom Account in stocks and bonds and real estate.

Retirement

The Freedom Plan has no specified retirement age. An individual can convert his Freedom Account into an annuity payable for life, at any time his combined Freedom Account, employer-provided pension, and other assets are adequate for retirement according to the individual's chosen life-style.

Other forms of annuity can be selected: joint and survivor annuities, life annuity with period certain guarantee, etc., according to the individual's needs and desires. The annuity can be adjusted for cost-of-living changes, to the extent its underlying assets are invested in Freedom Bonds. A portion of the Freedom Account can be taken in a lump sum at retirement. Some restrictions may be advisable to assure that a minimum pension is payable for life.

Comment: The elimination of a retirement age arbitrarily fixed by the government, together with the added flexibility offered by the Freedom Plan (regarding the amounts saved for retirement, the way such amounts are invested, etc.), would be a major step in restoring control to the individual of important life decisions.

When benefits are paid from the Freedom Account, the assets will have to be sold or liquidated—gradually, not all at once. This is discussed in a later section entitled Financing and Transition Cost.

It is presumed that the retirement benefits will be paid by the government, which will thus be acting as an insurance company. Alternatively, at retirement, the amount in an individual's Freedom Account could be transferred to a commercial insurance company that would then make the retirement payments. If these payments are adjusted for inflation, however, the insurer would, as a practical matter, have to invest the assets underlying the annuity in Inflation-Linked Treasury Bonds similar to Freedom Bonds.

Medical Care

Upon retirement, most individuals will want and need some form of medical insurance. In fact, such insurance should be required unless complete financial independence can be proved. Monthly premiums for such insurance can be withheld from the monthly retirement benefit paid from the Freedom Account. Whether the insurance is Medicare (in whatever form it may exist from time to time) or comparable private commercial insurance, the full cost of such insurance will be paid by the individual receiving the medical insurance.

Comment: The present method of financing Medicare is unworkable. Under the HI program an individual pays an HI tax during his working years and then in his retirement years receives HI benefits that bear absolutely no relationship to such taxes. The SMI program is more logical: No tax is paid during an individual's working years, but, when an individual becomes eligible, he elects the optional SMI coverage and pays a premium (withheld from his retirement benefit). When the SMI program began, an individual paid 50 percent of the cost, with the balance paid from general revenue. Currently, an individual pays only about 25 percent of the SMI cost. In future years under present law, an individual will pay, on average, only about 8 percent of the SMI cost. With most of the SMI cost paid by general revenue (that is, by "someone else"), there is no incentive for beneficiaries and physicians to control the cost—thus, it is in a steady upward spiral.

Disability

If an individual becomes disabled, the amount in his Freedom Account can be used to provide a disability annuity. A person may want additional disability benefits, particularly in the early years of the buildup of the Freedom Account. This can be done by purchasing an appropriately designed disability insurance policy from a commercial insurance company, and the premiums would be paid from the Freedom Account.

Death

If a person dies before beginning to collect a retirement annuity, the amount in the Freedom Account will be used to pay benefits to his survivors or estate. An individual may want additional death benefits, particularly in the early years of the buildup of the Freedom Account. This can be done by purchasing an appropriately designed life insurance policy from a commercial insurance company; the premiums would be paid from the Freedom Account.

Comment: If, for any reason, commercial insurance companies do not make available appropriately designed life insurance and disability insurance policies to all who apply for them, the government could offer this insurance—either through the Social Security Administration or a specially designed agency.

A strong case can be made for requiring an individual to purchase some minimum level of life insurance and disability insurance (which would depend on the size of his Freedom Account, employer-provided insurance, etc.). This would be an effective way of minimizing welfare cases.

Taxation

All individual contributions to the Freedom Account after January 1, 2000, will be deductible from gross income for purposes of determining federal income tax. Employer contributions to the Freedom Account will be deductible in determining employer taxes and will not be taxable currently to the employee.

When an amount is withdrawn from the Freedom Account upon retirement, disability, or death, it will be subject to federal income taxation. Amounts withdrawn from the Freedom Account to purchase life insurance, disability insurance, or health insurance, will not be subject to taxation. The tax treatment of benefits payable by life, disability, or health insurance will be determined by the government as part of its overall tax policy.

Comment: Individual contributions to the Freedom Account will be tax deductible, whereas individual taxes paid under the Social Security system were not tax deductible. Therefore, the current out-of-pocket cost to the individual will be lower under the Freedom Plan.

The above tax treatment is theoretically incorrect with respect to individual Social Security contributions made prior to January 1, 2000, since these contributions were not tax deductible yet will be subjected to tax when ultimately received as benefits. An adjustment for this fact could be made or it could be ignored.

Financing and Transition Cost

Any discussion of the financing of the Freedom Plan and the transition provisions to such a plan tends to be confusing, just as any discussion of the financing of the present system can be confusing. And those who oppose reform can deliberately make it more confusing so as to stymie change.

Here is one way to think of the financial consequences of the new plan proposed in this chapter. There are two groups of participants: the older group who will continue to receive the benefits provided under the present plan, and the younger group (those under age 55 on January 1, 2000) who will receive lower benefits than those provided under the present plan—even though they will receive full value for their actual past and future contributions. Since total benefits under the new plan will be less than those that would have been provided under the old plan, the new plan obviously costs less than the old plan.

Some people who oppose change in Social Security say that we cannot afford to pay for "future service benefits" under a new system and for "past service benefits" under the present system. They say that any change will result in some kind of burdensome "transition cost"; or that it will entail a "double cost" because we must pay for the new plan and pay off the liability for benefits accrued under the present plan. This is an absurd argument. There is no "transition cost." Just because we use a different method to define and finance future service benefits, that does not increase the cost or the liability for the past service benefits under the present system. In fact, as noted earlier, the liability for past service benefits would be lower under the Freedom Plan than under the present system, with respect to participants under age 55 on the date of change.

When benefits become payable—whether it is to participants who continued in the old Social Security

plan or to participants in the new Freedom Plan—
some of the trust fund's investments must be sold.
The sale of stocks, real estate, mutual funds, etc., is
straightforward. The sale of either treasury bonds or
Freedom Bonds is more complicated since it
requires that the government somehow find the
money to redeem those bonds. This money can
come from any one, or a combination, of the following sources:

- New contributions under the Freedom Plan
  that are used to buy Freedom Bonds (as distinguished from contributions that are invested
  otherwise) are automatically loaned to the government and are thus available to redeem the
  existing bonds. In other words, in order to pay
  current benefits, the government can borrow
  from current contributions to the Freedom
  Plan, just as it has borrowed in the past from
  current Social Security taxpayers. However,
  there won't be as much money to borrow in the
  future as in the past.
- The government can issue new treasury bonds
  to the public and use the proceeds to redeem
  the existing bonds.
- The government can reduce its spending, yet
  continue the same level of tax collection, and use
  the excess taxes to redeem the existing bonds.
- The government can collect additional general
  revenue and use the increased tax income to
  redeem the existing bonds.

Accordingly, the government will have consider-
able flexibility in determining how to redeem the
treasury bonds and the Freedom Bonds representing

past service benefits. Through continued borrowing, the government can even freeze the liability for
past service benefits at its current level. Of course,
it would be better for the nation's future economy
if the government would reduce spending, borrow
less, and start paying off the tremendous debt it has
created in the process of operating a Social Security
system that is financially unsound. But it is not necessary to do this in order to adopt a revised system
such as the Freedom Plan.

People who use high "transition costs" as an
excuse for not revising the Social Security system
are worried about two things. Social Security will
not be able to keep borrowing the full amount of
future Social Security contributions in order to pay
current benefits; and the extent of the liability for
past service benefits will become obvious. This will
force the system to operate on a more financially
sound basis. Heaven forbid!

Freedom of Choice: Good or Bad?

The Freedom Plan would give the taxpayer more
control over his financial future. He would have
some say in how part of his Freedom Account was
invested. He would make decisions about the kinds
of disability insurance, life insurance, and health
insurance to buy. He would be able to retire any
time his financial circumstances made it possible,
without interference by government regulations.

Most people want this increased control over
their lives. Of course, increased control means
increased responsibility. And many social planners
and economists think the public is not capable of

making these personal decisions. (They don't admit this openly for fear of offending you.)

Here's the basic question: Should we set up systems (Social Security, as well as a host of other institutions) that assume that no one is capable of making life decisions or of being responsible for himself and his family and thereby lower the average level of national competence? Or should we set up systems that assume that everyone is capable of being responsible for himself and his family, thus raising the average level of national competence, and make "safety net" provisions for those who fail?

When the Soviet Union collapsed a few years ago, we heard heartrending stories about the difficulty people were having in making simple (to us) decisions about managing their personal lives. Of course, the government had made such decisions for them for nearly fifty years—two whole generations. I witnessed this same phenomenon twenty-five years ago while serving on an International Executive Service Corps assignment in West Africa. During colonial rule, the Africans were completely subservient to their colonial masters and were neither allowed nor taught to make important decisions. Naturally, when independence came, the people were not prepared to be independent.

If you don't want more control over your lives; if you don't want the responsibility that goes with that control; if you don't want the opportunity to be wildly successful but possibly fail; then sit back and relax and the "government" will take care of you. Just remember what Hillary Clinton recently said to the press (as quoted in Chapter 1):

> When Franklin Roosevelt proposed Social
> Security, he didn't go out selling it with actu-
> arial tables. . . . He basically said, "Look, here's
> the deal: You pay; you're taken care of; you
> have social security in your old age."

Remember, also, that under Social Security the
government has not assumed any obligation to provide benefits in old age. Rather, it has tried to
impose that obligation on future generations of
taxpayers—who may not be willing and able to
assume such an unaffordable obligation, which
they played no role in designing.

During the past twenty years, Americans have
devoted a great deal of time and energy to studying
and worrying about Social Security. The concerns
are real, not artificial, and indicate that there are
serious problems underlying the design of Social
Security. The public can no longer be tranquilized by
The Big Lie, or by public relations campaigns about
how good Social Security is; it is time to develop solutions to the problems.

There is no reason for this country to continue
with a social insurance system that is so controver-
sial and unpopular and whose financial status must
constantly be debated. Living with such a system is
an unnecessary drain on our collective productivity
and psyche. It is eminently more sensible for us to
design a social insurance system that is understood
and perceived as fair and reasonable by the majority of the citizens—one that will support rather than
hinder the attainment of a healthy and productive

national economy. But this will never happen until we oust the politicians who tell us lies and we elect the politicians who will tell us the truth. Your fate and the fate of your children are in your hands.

10

Personal Financial Planning

*He who would be well taken care of must
take care of himself.*
— W. G. Sumner

This book is devoted to explaining the present
Social Security system and the need to change it,
and it is a plea for you to get involved with making
change happen. In short, the book is calling on you
to be a good citizen for the benefit of your own and
later generations.

But what about your own personal financial security? At best it will be several years before significant
changes are made in Social Security so that the system can be considered a stable program that can be
depended on to keep its long-range promises. It is
natural, therefore, that many people ask: What
should I do now to provide for my own personal
financial security in the event of sickness, death, disability, or old age?

Without meaning to be facetious, my first bit of
advice is to find some career or line of work you
enjoy, because you will probably be doing it longer
than you think you will.

The second thing to do is realize that Social Security was never intended to meet all your financial needs and it never will. Under the present program, as well as any revised program, it is necessary for you to supplement Social Security. To protect your family from financial stress, you must first compare what you need with what you have—much easier to say than to do. If you provide the principal financial support for your family, define your needs and those of your family in the event of your sickness, disability, death, or retirement. Be specific about the amount of income needed and how long it will be required. Do the same for other family members who provide financial support. Also define the needs that will arise if a member of your family becomes sick or disabled.

Then analyze all the programs that will provide benefits in any of those events: Social Security and other government programs; job-related, fringe-benefit plans; personal insurance and saving; and so forth. Find out what benefits will be provided by each of these programs. A surprising number of unmet needs will be revealed. In some cases there may be duplications in benefit protection. You can then set about to fill the gaps in protection and to eliminate the duplications.

This comparison of what you have with what you need in the way of financial protection will require a lot of effort by you or your financial advisor. The Social Security Administration will provide, upon request, estimates of benefits payable upon retirement, disability, or death. (For further information, phone 1-800-772-1213 and request a Personal

Earnings and Benefit Estimate Statement, Form
SSA-7004.) Of course you will have to take these
estimates with a grain of salt, particularly if you are
a member of the baby boom generation or
Generation X. The personnel department of your
employer can usually give information about
employer-provided benefits (group life insurance,
disability and sickness benefits, retirement benefits,
etc.) and may or may not be equipped to provide
detailed information about Social Security benefits.
Your employer may also be able to give you information about benefits under programs it does not
directly administer, such as workers' compensation
and state cash-sickness plans. Your life insurance
agent can provide information about any individual
life insurance, disability insurance, health insurance, or retirement policies you may have. Putting
all this information together is not an easy matter,
but it is something you must do if you are to meet
your various needs and those of your family on the
most economical basis possible.

Where do you start? You may want to work with a
financial advisor—a relatively new breed of consultant
specializing in the analysis of your total financial picture. There are several financial planning organizations that recognize the qualifications of their members with professional designations: e.g., Certified
Financial Planner (CFP), and Registered Financial
Planner (RFP). Some life insurance agents are quali-
fied to help you organize your financial affairs. You
stand a better chance with an experienced, well-
trained agent—perhaps one who has completed one
of the study programs offered by the American

College in Bryn Mawr, Pennsylvania, and has thus earned the designation of Chartered Life Underwriter (CLU) or Chartered Financial Consultant (ChFc) or Master of Sciences in Financial Services (MSFC). Some CPAs have earned the credential of Accredited Personal Financial Specialist.

It is reasonable to expect your employer—probably through the personnel department—to provide some help in comparing your financial needs with the coverage offered under employer-provided plans. In the end, however, despite help from these advisors, you must get heavily involved and do much of the work yourself. Perhaps this is as it should be. Your family financial situation is a unique and personal matter, and you cannot expect a stranger to have the same level of interest as you.[1]

Appendix A:
Comparison of Projected Expenditures and Tax Income

The following comments will consider separately the different parts of Social Security: the monthly cash benefits (the old-age, survivors, and disability benefits); and the Medicare benefits (Hospital Insurance and Supplementary Medical Insurance).

Chart A.1 compares the projected income and outgo for the cash benefits part of Social Security, based on the 1996 Trustees Reports. Future projections are shown under three alternative sets of demographic and economic assumptions, considered by the Trustees to indicate the range within which future costs will probably fall. The intermediate-cost projections are used by the government for planning purposes and for all pronouncements on the financial condition of Social Security. My personal opinion is that the actual future cost will be closer to the high-cost projections; and that the low-cost projections are so unrealistically optimistic as to be worthless. Moreover, if the benefits provided by

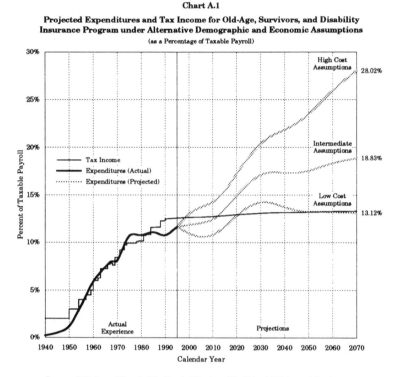

Chart A.1

Projected Expenditures and Tax Income for Old-Age, Survivors, and Disability Insurance Program under Alternative Demographic and Economic Assumptions

(as a Percentage of Taxable Payroll)

Source: *1996 Annual Report of the Board of Trustees of the Federal Old-Age and Survivors Insurance and Disability Insurance Trust Funds.*

Social Security are to be considered firm promises (as most people seem to assume they are), the program should be set up in such a way that it would be viable under the so-called high-cost assumptions.

As shown in Chart A.1, the present OASDI combined employee/employer tax rate of 12.4 percent will have to rise to between 19 percent and 28 percent of taxable earnings during the lifetime of those entering the work force today, if there are no changes in benefits (based, respectively, on the

Chart A.2

Projected Expenditures and Tax Income for Hospital Insurance Program under Alternative Demographic and Economic Assumptions

(as a Percentage of Taxable Payroll)

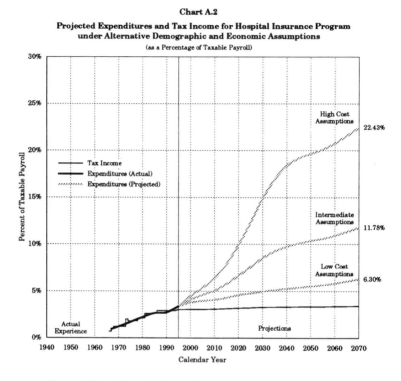

Source: *1996 Annual Report of the Board of Trustees of the Federal Hospital Insurance Trust Fund.*

intermediate- and high-cost projections). Taxable earnings per year are limited to $62,700 per worker in 1996, rising in future years as the nation's average earnings increase.

Chart A.2 compares the projected income and outgo for the Hospital Insurance part of Social Security, also based on the 1996 Trustees Reports. These projections are shown as a percentage of total payroll with no upper limit, since the HI tax applies to all earnings. Total payroll is currently

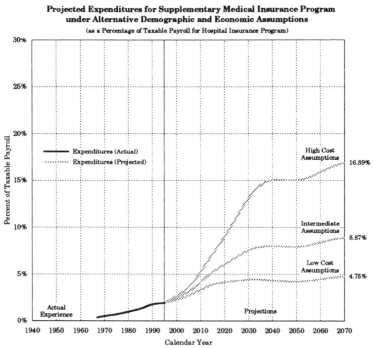

Chart A.3

Projected Expenditures for Supplementary Medical Insurance Program under Alternative Demographic and Economic Assumptions

(as a Percentage of Taxable Payroll for Hospital Insurance Program)

Note: Projected SMI income is not shown. By law, income from beneficiary premiums and government general revenue contributions are automatically increased each year to meet projected expenditures.

Source: *1996 Annual Report of the Board of Trustees of the Federal Supplementary Medical Insurance Trust Fund* and unpublished data from the Office of the Actuary, Health Care Financing Administration.

about 20 percent higher than the taxable payroll for the cash benefits part of Social Security.

Chart A.2 indicates that the present combined employee/employer tax rate of 2.9 percent will have to rise to between 12 percent and 22 percent of taxable earnings during the lifetime of those entering the work force today, if the benefits and financing method are not revised.

Chart A.3 shows the projected outgo for the Supplementary Medical Insurance part of Social Security, based on the 1996 Trustees Reports. The income to the SMI program has not been shown on the chart. Beneficiaries currently pay "premiums" equal to approximately 25 percent of the total SMI cost, and the remaining 75 percent of the cost is paid by general revenue; however, under present law these premiums are projected to decrease in future years (relative to total cost) and will average less than 10 percent of the total cost. The projected outgo is shown as a percentage of taxable payroll for Hospital Insurance purposes, to facilitate comparison of outgo under the HI and SMI programs. Chart A.3 indicates that expenditures will rise from their current level of 2 percent to between 9 percent and 17 percent of such payroll during the lifetime of those entering the work force today.

The preceding three charts make it clear that:

- Benefit costs have risen steadily in the past; and, of course, tax income has risen accordingly.
- Hospital Insurance costs began to exceed tax income in 1992 and the deficit is projected to grow rapidly under all three projections.
- For the Old-Age, Survivors, and Disability Insurance program, tax income will be sufficient to pay benefits for the next few years, but about the time the baby boom generation begins to reach age 65 in the year 2011, benefit costs will begin to exceed tax income by ever-increasing amounts.

Accordingly, it is not a question of whether we should take action to restore balance to income and outgo under the various parts of Social Security. It is only a question of how and when—and the sooner the better.

Appendix B:
Names and Addresses of
Selected National Officials

If you want to write a letter to the President, to your own Senators and Representatives, or to others, expressing your personal concerns about Social Security, including Medicare, this appendix may be useful. It includes sample letters for your guidance; however, an original letter in your own words might be more effective. If you receive a particularly interesting response (for example, one that says "Don't worry, be happy"), please send me a copy.

The sample letters illustrate how to address the President, a Senator, and a Representative. All Senators have the same address, and all Representatives have the same address.

The heads of the Social Security Administration and the Health Care Financing Administration (which administers Medicare) are as follows:

The Honorable Shirley S. Chater*
Commissioner
Social Security Administration
Room 900, Altmeyer Building
6401 Security Boulevard
Baltimore, Maryland 21235

The Honorable Bruce C. Vladeck
Administrator
Health Care Financing
  Administration
7500 Security Boulevard
Baltimore, Maryland 21244

The Board of Trustees was established under the Social Security Act to oversee the financial operations of the trust funds (OASDI, HI, and SMI). The Board is composed of six members. Four members serve by virtue of their positions in the Federal Government: the Secretary of the Treasury who is the Managing Trustee, the Secretary of Labor, the Secretary of Health and Human Services, and the Commissioner of Social Security. The other two members are appointed by the President and confirmed by the Senate to serve as Public Trustees. Stephen G. Kellison and Marilyn Moon are currently serving four-year terms that began on July 20, 1995. The Social Security Act requires that the Board of Trustees report to the Congress annually on the financial and actuarial status of each of the trust funds.

Ex-Officio Trustees

The Honorable Robert E. Rubin
Managing Trustee
Secretary of the Treasury
Main Treasury Building
15th St. and Pennsylvania
  Ave., NW
Washington, DC 20220

The Honorable Alexis Herman
Secretary of Labor
200 Constitution Ave., NW
Washington, DC 20210

*Mrs. Chater resigned effective as of January 31, 1997, and her replacement had not been announced as this book went to press.

The 1994 legislation that made the Social Security Administration an independent agency also created a Social Security Advisory Board. The law provides for a bipartisan, seven-member Advisory Board, three members of which are to be appointed by the President, with two each being appointed by the Speaker of the House and the President pro tempore of the Senate. This board advises the Commissioner of Social Security on policies related to the Old-Age, Survivors, and Disability Insurance programs, and to the Supplemental Security Income program (administered by the Social Security Administration but financed by general revenue). The board convened for the first time in February 1996. Members serve for five years.

*Mrs. Chater resigned effective as of January 31, 1997, and her replacement had not been announced as this book went to press.

Social Security Advisory Board Members

Harlan Mathews (Chairman)
Farris, Mathews, Gilman, Branan, & Hellen, P.L.C.
511 Union Street, Suite 2400
Nashville, Tennessee 37219

William Brooks
Vice President of Corporate
  Relations
General Motors Corporation
3044 West Grand
Detroit, Michigan 48202

Lori L. Hansen
Policy Analyst
National Academy of
  Social Insurance
11871 Snowfield Court
Traverse City, Michigan
49686

Martha Keys
Vice President for Public Affairs
National Multiple Sclerosis Society
733 Third Avenue #500
New York, New York 10017-5706

Gerald Shea
Assistant to the President
AFL-CIO
815 16th Street, NW
Washington, DC 20006

Arthur L. "Pete" Singleton*
Consultant on Government
Box 158
Dunnsville, Virginia 22454

Carolyn L. Weaver
Director, Social Security
  and Pension Project
American Enterprise
  Institute
1150 17th Street, NW
Washington, DC 20036

*Mr. Singleton resigned in November, 1996 to become majority chief of staff in the House of Representatives, and his replacement had not been announced as this book went to press.

Sample Letter #1

President Bill Clinton
The White House
1600 Pennsylvania Avenue
Washington, DC 20500

Dear Mr. President:

Social Security and Medicare are an important part of every retired person's livelihood. Actuarial projections contained in the latest official Trustees Reports indicate that future tax income will not be adequate to provide the future benefits that have been promised during my lifetime, much less during the lifetime of my children. Accordingly, substantial cuts in benefits or increases in taxes, or both, are inevitable.

I urge you to look into this matter and make appropriate changes *now*, not years from now at the last minute when it will be too late for orderly reforms. Planning for retirement is a long-range process, and last-minute reductions in Social Security and Medicare benefits are not acceptable.

For your guidance I suggest that you read Chapters 8 and 9 of the book *The Big Lie: What Every Baby Boomer Should Know About Social Security and Medicare*, written by A. Haeworth Robertson, a former Chief Actuary of the Social Security Administration. [This paragraph is optional, of course. You may have a reform plan of your own to recommend.]

I look forward to an early response to my concerns about Social Security, including Medicare.

Sincerely yours,

Sample Letter #2

The Honorable _____
U.S. Senate
Washington, DC 20510

Dear Senator _____:
   I am a baby boomer who will reach age 65 in the year 2020. I am trying to make financial plans for my retirement and would like to know whether I can count on receiving Social Security and Medicare at the levels currently being promised.
   The latest Trustees Reports state that in 1992 the Hospital Insurance program began paying out more than it collected in payroll taxes; and that in the year 2012 (eight years before I reach age 65), the OASDI program will start paying out more than it collects in payroll taxes. Furthermore, this financial problem will get worse as more and more of my generation retires.
   When is Congress going to stop denying that there is a problem, and fix the system? How can I have confidence in a government that is unwilling to look beyond the next election when making plans that will affect my financial future?
   May I suggest that you read Chapters 8 and 9 of the book, *The Big Lie: What Every Baby Boomer Should Know About Social Security and Medicare*, written by A. Haeworth Robertson, a former Chief Actuary of the Social Security Administration. This book discusses the magnitude of the problems that lie ahead and proposes a solution that seems reasonable to me. [This paragraph is optional.]
   I look forward to an early response to my concerns about Social Security, including Medicare.
   Sincerely yours,

Sample Letter #3

The Honorable _____
U.S. House of Representatives
Washington, DC 20515

Dear Congressman _____:
    Enclosed is a copy of an interesting new book I have just read, *The Big Lie: What Every Baby Boomer Should Know About Social Security and Medicare*. It was written by A. Haeworth Robertson, a former Chief Actuary of the Social Security Administration. In 1981 he wrote *The Coming Revolution in Social Security*, which correctly anticipated all the problems that Social Security and Medicare are now beginning to experience.

    I hope you will give this new book careful consideration. Some of the ideas expressed in the book may be useful as Congress debates the inevitable Social Security and Medicare reforms.

    Please let me know if you plan to play an active role in making Social Security and Medicare more dependable. The uncertainty about these programs does little to inspire confidence in the government.

    Sincerely yours,

Sample Letter #4

Friend or Colleague

Dear _____:

Enclosed is a copy of an interesting new book I have just read, *The Big Lie: What Every Baby Boomer Should Know About Social Security and Medicare*. It was written by A. Haeworth Robertson, a former Chief Actuary of the Social Security Administration. In 1981 he wrote *The Coming Revolution in Social Security*, which correctly anticipated all the problems that Social Security and Medicare are now beginning to experience.

Many of us have long suspected that the Social Security and Medicare promises made to Baby Boomers were unrealistic and could not be fulfilled. This book confirms our worst suspicions. Even more aggravating, this information about the need for reform has been available for years and our politicians have ignored it— right up through the 1996 Presidential Elections.

I hope you will read this book and get angry enough to become active in helping design a Social Security system for our generation and our children's generation that is workable, affordable, and dependable.

Recommend this book to your friends (still better, buy a few copies and give them away). Don't vote for any more politicians who tell us, "Don't Worry, Be Happy." If an aroused public could help stop the Vietnam War, surely we can reform the Social Security system.

Sincerely,

(Obviously, this letter is just an illustrative sample and will not necessarily reflect your personal views. Write a letter that *does* reflect your personal views and get active in securing your financial future.)

Appendix C: Extraordinary Popular Delusions and the Madness of Crowds

A Luncheon Address by A. Haeworth Robertson to the Middle Atlantic Actuarial Club in Annapolis, Maryland on September 12, 1991

The individual human mind is extraordinary. When used in a free and creative and daring way it can produce miracles. Think of the achievements of Albert Einstein or Thomas Edison or the Wright Brothers. Or Mohandas Gandhi or Mother Theresa. The human mind can also produce horror and destruction: witness Adolf Hitler and Joseph Stalin.

The collective state of mind of the crowd is an important determinant of whether an idea is accepted or rejected—of whether mankind progresses or regresses.

Astronomy: Copernicus and Galileo

Nicolaus Copernicus was born in Poland in 1473. He worked for years developing his hypothesis that the planets revolve around the sun. In contrast,

Ptolemy—and the Church—maintained the geocentric theory that the planets revolve around the earth. (Otherwise, how could the earth, where we all live, be the **center** of the universe?)

By age 40, Copernicus was convinced that he was right, but he hesitated to publish his ideas for fear of difficulties with the Church. Finally, in his late 60s, Copernicus decided to publish his theories, and on May 24, 1543, at age 70, he received the first copy of his book from the printer. He died that same day.

Twenty-one years later, Galileo was born in Pisa. By about age 40 he had decided that Copernicus was correct, but he could not prove it until several years later when he improved upon the telescope, invented earlier in Holland. Thereafter, he taught the Copernican heliocentric theory until ordered by the Church in 1616 to refrain from such heretical teaching.

Seven years later when the Pope died and a more open-minded one was installed, Galileo was led to believe that it was acceptable to the Church to resume his teaching. In 1632, he published the *Dialogue Concerning the Two Chief World Systems*, his most famous work, which supported the Copernican theory. The Church brought Galileo to trial before the Inquisition of Rome and required him to publicly recant his view that the earth moved around the sun and thus was not the center of the universe. This the 69-year-old scientist did in open court. He died 9 years later at age 78.

It is tempting to say that Copernicus and Galileo were the victims of narrow-minded thinking in the

16th and 17th centuries and that those days are past. Unfortunately, those days may not really be past.

Air Power and General Billy Mitchell

During World War I, General Billy Mitchell was an outstanding U.S. combat air commander. After the war, he became rather outspoken in his prophecies about strategic bombardment, mass airborne operations, the strategic importance of Alaska and the polar regions, and the eclipse of the battleship by the airplane. He was a strong proponent of an independent air force and of unified control of air power, both of which were opposed by the U.S. Army general staff and the U.S. Navy.

In December 1925 an army court-martial convicted General Mitchell of insubordination and suspended his rank and duty for 5 years. He died 11 years later at age 56.

In 1948, after World War II had proved his heretical views to be correct, and 23 years after his court-martial, and 12 years after his death, Mitchell was vindicated: the chief of staff of the newly created U.S. Air Force presented to Mitchell's son a special medal authorized by the U.S. Congress in Mitchell's honor.

Oh yes, there is one more idea General Mitchell expressed. In 1924, the year before his court-martial, he predicted that Japan would attack Pearl Harbor—17 years before it happened. He outlined the attack in detail and wrote that it would be made with airplanes launched from specially designed ships "equipped with a flying-off deck."

Copernicus and Galileo and Mitchell are just a few examples of individuals who were correct but who were not believed. There are, of course, many examples of individuals—and crowds—who were incorrect but who **were** believed, much to the regret of the believers.

The Dutch Tulip Craze

Tulips were introduced into western Europe about the middle of the 16th century. They were imported from Constantinople, the word *tulip* having been derived from the Turkish word for *turban*.

The Dutch fondness for tulips developed into a mania—a madness of the crowds. Huge profits were being made in trading tulips. Everyone imagined that the passion for tulips would last forever, and that the wealthy from every part of the world would send to Holland for tulips and pay whatever prices were asked for them. They imagined that the riches of Europe would be concentrated on the shores of the Zuider Zee and that poverty would be banished from the favored clime of Holland. Nobles, citizens, farmers, mechanics, seamen, footmen, maidservants, even chimney sweeps and old clotheswomen dabbled in tulips. People of all grades converted their property into cash and invested it in flowers.

A single root of the rare species of tulip called the Viceroy was traded in exchange for the following items valued at 2,500 florins:

Item	Florins
Two lasts of wheat	448
Four lasts of rye	558
Four fat oxen	480
Eight fat swine	240

Twelve fat sheep	120
Two hogsheads of wine	70
Four tuns of beer	32
Two tuns of butter	192
One thousand lbs. of cheese	120
A complete bed	100
A suit of clothes	80
A silver drinking cup	60
Total	2,500

And then, in November 1636, the end came as the more prudent people began to see that this folly could not last forever. Prices plummeted by 90 percent. The people sought government help in enforcing tulip trading contracts, but the judges unanimously refused to interfere—on the grounds that the debts contracted in gambling were not debts in law.

Consensus is Not Synonymous With Verity

The earth is **not** flat, it is round.

The planets revolve around the sun, **not** around the earth.

The development of air power **was** inevitable. On December 7, 1941, the Japanese **did** attack Pearl Harbor.

Insurance companies **can** fail if they are not managed properly.

Employers **can** fail to keep their pension and health care promises if the promises are unaffordable or if suitable advance provision is not made.

The Congress **can** promise more in Social Security benefits to baby boomers than the children of the baby boomers will be willing and able to pay for.

State and local governments **can** make financial decisions that will result in financial failure.

The U.S. government **can** make financial decisions that will impoverish future generations rather than enrich them.

Just because a lot of people are doing it, that doesn't make it right. Just because a lot of people believe it, that doesn't make it true. **Consensus is not synonymous with verity.**

Dare to Challenge the Status Quo

It is difficult to challenge the status quo. It is uncomfortable for those being challenged as well as for the challenger. People do not like uncertainty, and they fear the unknown. Accordingly, people resist change from the existing state of affairs because it entails uncertainty and the unknown.

A significant amount of tradition, with its continuity and predictability, is necessary for a smoothly functioning society; however, absolute and unquestioned tradition will not let us discover the truth.

If you believe that something is not right, that it is not rational, I urge you to say so. You will have plenty of opportunities to do this in matters large and small. The difficulty is not to discover senseless acts and ideas—they abound. The difficulty is to find ways to challenge and expose these senseless acts and ideas, but at the same time to create minimum discomfort for yourself and for those who have a vested interest or who are afraid of change.

Actuaries, with their unique training, experience, and perspective can—if they will—help people make responsible financial decisions about future events.

Actuaries can—if they will—help people lead a better life in the future.

I urge you to seek the truth, to challenge the status quo. Because of your actuarial training and experience, you are equipped to see truths that others cannot easily see.

Deceit and hypocrisy and mediocrity are contagious, and I fear we are approaching an epidemic stage. But there is an antidote: honesty and sincerity and excellence—and they are also contagious.

Use your mind and your power of reason to the utmost. Be extraordinary. Do your part to dispel the popular delusions and the madness of crowds.

◆   ◆   ◆   ◆   ◆   ◆

It's the action, not the fruit of the action, that's important. You have to do the right thing. It may not be in your power, may not be in your time, that there'll be any fruit. But that doesn't mean you stop doing the right thing. You may never know what results come from your action. But if you do nothing, there will be no result.

— Mohandas K. Gandhi
Quoting from a Hindu treatise

References

Davis, Burke. *The Billy Mitchell Affair*. New York: Random House, 1967.

Hart, Michael H. *The 100—A Ranking of the Most Influential Persons in History*. New York: Hart Publishing Company, Inc., 1978.

Mackay, Charles. *Extraordinary Popular Delusions and the Madness of Crowds*. New York: Farrar, Straus and Giroux, 1932. (Originally published in 1841 by Richard Bentley, New Burlington Street, London.)

Appendix D:
Will Anarchy or Socialism Result from Social Security's Future Broken Promises?

A Commentary by A. Haeworth Robertson originally based upon the book Social Security: What Every Taxpayer Should Know, *but modified to reflect information in the 1996 Trustees Reports*

Social Security is a program of future promises. It is a program of two separate and distinct kinds of promise: one promise that specified benefits will be paid to the inactive segment of the population; and another promise that specified taxes will be collected from the active segment of the population. These are benefit promises to one generation and taxation promises to that generation's children.

Both promises are equally important, but, unfortunately, we have tended to place more emphasis on our promises to the inactive population than to the active population. We have placed more emphasis on the benefit promises than on the taxation promises.

Under a pay-as-you-go system of benefits based on social adequacy instead of individual equity, there is virtually no relationship between benefit promises and the taxation promises made to an individual or to a group.

Some would argue that there **is** a connection between benefits and taxes because the system is partially advance funded. This is false; the system is not, in reality, advance funded at all. The government immediately spends any Social Security taxes it receives that are not required for current benefits, and then states its intention to replace this money, with interest, by collecting general revenue in the future when it is needed to pay benefits. This is clearly not advance funding, government rhetoric to the contrary notwithstanding.

Some would argue that a particular generation pays taxes during its working lifetime that are equivalent to the benefits it will receive; that a generation buys and pays for its own benefits. This is false. Social Security, by its very nature, does not provide an individual or an entire generation with benefits equivalent to taxes paid.

Benefit promises and taxation promises are separate and distinct promises made to separate and distinct groups of people, with a certain amount of overlapping. Therein lies the crux of the Social Security problem.

Benefit Promises vs. Taxation Promises

What promises have we made and can we keep them? The latest Trustees Reports (1996) contain the projected cost of our benefit promises that are intended to be financed primarily by the Social Security payroll tax: the Old-Age, Survivors, Disability, and Hospital Insurance programs.

The cost is projected to rise from its current level of 15% of covered, taxable payroll to between 28% and 43% of such payroll by the middle of the next century (depending on whether you accept the intermediate- or the high-cost projections). I give no credence whatsoever to the low-cost projections and believe the so-called high-cost projections are the appropriate ones to assess whether or not we can fulfill our benefit promises.

What level of taxes have we promised future generations that they will have to pay to finance those benefits? We have promised that current payroll tax rates will continue indefinitely: namely 7.65% from employees and 7.65% from employers. In addition, general revenue that is equivalent to approximately 1% of payroll will be generated (principally from taxation of Social Security benefits). This taxation promise will be sufficient to finance only 45% to 65% of the benefit promises we have made to the baby boom generation (based, respectively, on the high-cost and intermediate projections).

In addition, of course, is the promise to provide Supplementary Medical Insurance benefits. The cost of SMI is projected to rise by mid-21st century from its current level of 2% of payroll to 8% of payroll based on the intermediate projections, and 15% of payroll based on the high-cost projections.

The taxation promise for SMI is a little murky. Currently, approximately 25% of the cost of SMI is paid by "premiums" from persons eligible for benefit protection and the remaining 75% is drawn from general revenue.

It would seem that the taxation promise is that taxpayers must pay whatever amount of general revenue is needed in the future, in addition to the "premiums," to provide SMI benefits; but the taxpayer has not been informed of this obligation. The 1996 SMI Trustees Reports do indicate that, based on the intermediate projections, the SMI cost will rise from 0.92% of the Gross Domestic Product in 1995 to 3.79% 75 years hence.

Which Promises Will Be Broken?

It is indisputable that some of Social Security's promises will be broken. The questions are which promises, when, how, and for what group of the population.

From Social Security's financial standpoint, there is little need to break either benefit promises or taxation promises during the next five years or so. Social Security's income and outgo will approximately balance during that period (assuming the total income is reallocated among the various parts of the program).

But beginning around the year 2006 when the first baby boomer reaches age 60, we shall have to renege on the promises. We can reduce benefits for the baby boomers, or we can increase taxes for the boomers still working as well as for all of the children of the boomers. I would submit that the choices we make will be much more significant and far-reaching than we can now envision.

Break the Taxation Promises

We could break the taxation promises and keep the benefit promises. People could continue to retire in their early 60s.

If we do this, one of the consequences would be very high Social Security taxes. During the 50 years from 2010 to 2060, combined tax rates paid by employees and employers, now 15.3%, would have to average about 25% based on the intermediate projections, and 35% based on the high-cost projections.

As burdensome as these taxes may be, they could probably be paid, but there is another important factor to consider. One of the underlying causes of the high future Social Security taxes will be the demographic shift in the ratio of workers to non-workers. In 1950, there were 16 active workers for every Social Security benefit recipient; today, the ratio is about 3 to 1; and in 2030 the ratio is projected to be 2 to 1 or lower. Just as a shift in this ratio results in high Social Security taxes for the remaining workers, it also results in higher taxes for everything else the working population normally supports.

Although such high taxes may be feasible, their assessment would have a marked effect on the standard of living of both the active and retired segments of the population. Active workers would obviously have less discretionary income; but there would also be fewer resources available for improved education, a cleaner environment, improved health care, a better maintained infrastructure of roads and bridges, and so forth.

In the future, it is unlikely that a work force consisting primarily of people less than age 65 would be large enough to produce all the goods and services needed to support the entire population. If they were able to do so, they would retain such a small proportion of what they produced, and there would be such a massive redistribution of income, that the nation would have moved a long way—if not all the way—toward a socialist economy.

And all of these consequences would flow not from deliberate decisions about how to allocate resources, but from:

- adopting a social insurance system in the 1930s that effectively divides the population into workers and non-workers;
- misrepresenting the nature of the system in order to gain public acceptance; and thus
- causing the public to consider the system to be inviolable and not subject to change to adjust for conditions unforeseen in the 1930s: namely, a baby boom followed by a baby bust, improved but more costly medical care, and longer life spans.

Break the Benefit Promises

We could break the benefit promises and keep the taxation promises. Benefits to baby boomers would have to be cut severely (35% based on the intermediate projections and 55% based on the high-cost projections). Obviously, people would not be able to retire as early as they had hoped and planned.

Because of the nature of Social Security's promises, the consequences of breaking those promises should not be underestimated. The Social Security program promises a certain level of retirement benefits in exchange for the payment of taxes during one's working years. Moreover, the Social Security Administration emphasizes that Social Security retirement benefits are not sufficient to replace the earnings lost through retirement, and it encourages workers to participate in private pension plans and to save and invest on their own in order to provide a total retirement income that will be sufficient for their needs. If, after several decades of playing by these rules, a worker is abruptly notified that Congress has chosen to reduce Social Security retirement benefits, then the worker may well be unable to adjust his or her own savings and pension to compensate for the lower Social Security benefits. The worker may then face the difficult choice of delaying retirement (if possible) or adjusting to a lower standard of living than planned.

Apart from the immediate impact on the retirement plans of the workers and their families, and the loss of public confidence in the Social Security program, such broken promises could have another serious ramification: namely, the complete loss of confidence in the government itself. Social Security is probably the last major government program in which the public still has any significant degree of confidence.

Without the confidence and support of the public, the institution of orderly government cannot long survive. If a major default occurs in Social Security benefit promises, anarchy may not be far behind.

Is There a Better Choice?

Is there a better choice than anarchy or socialism? It is probably unavoidable that we shall have a little of each, because the government has already waited too long to be honest with the public. The government has misrepresented the nature of Social Security and its long-range cost and implications for so long now that we cannot completely avoid the consequences. We can, however, minimize the adversity of those consequences with timely and well-chosen action.

There is no single best solution; the preferred solution depends upon one's objectives and philosophy. But whatever the solution may be, in order to minimize future turmoil it must have three characteristics:

- It must be decided upon and communicated to the public very soon—i.e., within the next two or three years—so that the baby boomers will have time to adjust their retirement plans.
- It must generally be considered fair, or at least an "equal sacrifice" among the various segments of the population.
- It must result in a more complete utilization of the nation's human resources over a longer proportion of each person's life.

The nation should provide an environment in which the capabilities of each individual can be utilized effectively, an environment that fosters meaningful activity, not empty idleness. Both the incentive and the opportunity should exist to enable individuals to work and produce throughout their lifetimes in a series of endeavors compatible with their changing physical and mental abilities. Government policies should be directed toward these goals and not toward the removal from the active work force of able-bodied persons—persons who must then be supported by the remaining active workers.

It will not be easy for the nation to move in this direction of full utilization of its human resources. The alternative will be continued high unemployment and underemployment, an ever-increasing pool of idle "disabled persons" and "aged persons," and a total cost to society that will be increasingly unbearable and that will eventually become destructive.

But before we can start developing solutions, more people must be aware that we have problems. And they must understand the nature and magnitude of the problems. A better understanding of Social Security is essential if it is to evolve into a system that will appropriately meet the needs of the baby boom generation, as well as ensuing generations, at a price that future taxpayers will be willing and able to pay.

Notes

Chapter 1

1. Reported in *Investors Business Daily*, October 20, 1994, page 1.

2. *44 Liquormart, Inc., et al. v. Rhode Island, et al.*, Case No. 94–1140, decided May 13, 1996.

3. This example is cited simply to indicate the power of the voters and not to be critical of the concept of catastrophic health insurance which, properly implemented, is desirable.

Chapter 2

1. Arthur M. Schlesinger, Jr., *The Age of Roosevelt*, vol. 2, "The Coming of the New Deal," Houghton-Mifflin, 1959, pp. 308–9.

2. This was the percentage of the retired population affected in 1995. Under present law, this percentage will increase each year in the future.

3. A. Haeworth Robertson, *Social Security: What Every Taxpayer Should Know*, The Retirement Policy Institute, Washington, DC, 1992, pp. 151–3.

4. Ibid., p. 121.

5. Ibid., Chapter 7, for a full discussion of the nature of this unfunded accrued liability.

Chapter 4

1. In fairness, it should be noted that Dr. Chater sometimes told the truth about Social Security's financial condition.

During the election campaign of 1996 she acknowledged publicly that to restore long-term financial balance to Social
Security, future benefits must be reduced or payroll taxes
increased. Rumor has it that she was thereupon informed by
the White House Chief of Staff that she could continue as
Commissioner of the Social Security Administration until election day, November 5, 1996. She subsequently resigned as of
January 31, 1997.

2. Third Millennium is a national non-profit and advocacy
organization started in 1993 by young Americans who are
deeply concerned about the country's future.

3. For a full discussion of the nature and consequences of
the "trust funds," see: A. Haeworth Robertson, *Social Security:
What Every Taxpayer Should Know*, The Retirement Policy
Institute, Washington, DC, 1992, Chapter 6.

Chapter 5

1. These examples are based on averages and ignore the
differences in male and female per capita medical care costs.

2. For a full discussion of this question, see: A. Haeworth
Robertson, *Social Security: What Every Taxpayer Should Know*,
The Retirement Policy Institute, Washington, DC, 1992,
Chapter 10.

3. For the OASDI and HI programs combined, all the trust
fund assets will be liquidated prior to the year 2010 under
both the intermediate projections and the high-cost projections; therefore, the bars depicting combined OASDI and HI
expenditures do not include a component for trust fund liquidation.

Chapter 7

1. Upon reading an early draft of this book, Frederick W.
Kilbourne, an actuary and long-time friend of mine, reminded me that in 1964 he wrote the following letter to the editor
of the Los Angeles Times-Mirror Company:

Millions of Americans are counting on two monthly checks to pay for their retirement years, one from their company pension plans and one from the Social Security System. The current funds under the former, together with expected future contributions on behalf of these people, are sufficient to provide the benefits promised. The current funds under the latter, together with expected future contributions on behalf of these people, are inadequate to provide the benefits promised. The current amount of this inadequacy, which is increasing all the time, is roughly equivalent to the national debt. Given a few more years, plus the inevitable liberalizations to the program which they will bring, there will be a trillion dollar deficit to sweep under the rug. Apparently our leaders feel that, if it only be big enough, a pyramid club need not fail. They are wrong.

The letter was published but the editor changed the reference to a "trillion dollar deficit" to read a "huge deficit."

Furthermore, there have been other actuaries, as well as a few non-actuaries, who have questioned the long-range financial stability of a pay-as-you-go social insurance system ever since its establishment in 1935.

Chapter 8

1. The situation for the Supplementary Medical Insurance part of Medicare is different. The law states that the gap between benefit outgo and premium income (currently, approximately 75 percent of the total cost) will be financed by general revenue, no matter how large the gap. In theory, SMI will never have a financing problem. In practice, however, a financing problem will arise when the government begins to have trouble raising the necessary general revenue. (This point appears to have been reached now, since the government is operating at a deficit and must borrow to obtain the funds necessary to operate.)

2. In 1987, Medicare benefit payments on behalf of persons aged 65 and older covered approximately 45 percent of their total medical expenses. (Daniel R. Waldo, Sally T. Sonnefeld, David R. McKusick, and Ross H. Arnett, III, "Health expenditures by age group, 1977 and 1987," *Health Care Financing Review*, Summer 1989.)

Chapter 9

1. This estimated liability is based on the intermediate-cost assumptions used by the Trustees and consists of about $6.3 trillion for Old Age, Survivors, and Disability Insurance benefits and $7.7 trillion for Medicare benefits ($4.4 trillion for Hospital Insurance and $3.3 trillion for Supplementary Medical Insurance). The amount included for Supplementary Medical Insurance represents the portion of the cost scheduled to be financed by general revenues; that is, not by participant premiums. Future modifications in the Medicare program could reduce this liability.

2. For example, according to a poll conducted by Public Opinion Strategies for the CATO Institute in 1996: 40 percent of the people surveyed believed that "The money you contribute to Social Security is credited to an account with your name on it."; and 33 percent believed that "When you retire, you only receive back the amount of money you put into Social Security plus interest."

3. Even the government—with all its experts—doesn't seem capable of understanding and administering Social Security benefits correctly. Consider the following excerpt from a news story in the October 5–6, 1996 edition of the *International Herald Tribune.*

Pensioners to Get Pinched Pennies
Los Angeles Times

WOODLAWN, Maryland—In a major computer snafu, the Social Security Administration has determined that 700,000 Americans have been shortchanged out of more than $850 million in retirement benefits since 1972, agency officials have disclosed.

Although the administration recognized two years ago that there was a glitch in its computers, only recently did it determine the full extent and complexity of the problem.

The agency already is making back payments of nearly $400 million to about 402,000 retirees. Social Security officials now estimate that 295,000 more as-yet-unknown recipients, all of whom continued to work after they began receiving Social Security benefits, are owed back benefits of an additional $450 million.

Since it took more than 20 years to discover this mistake, it might make you wonder if there are any other "undiscovered mistakes" and whether they will ever be discovered. Is it possible that Professor Milton Friedman, Nobel Laureate Economist, was right when he said, "The Social Security system has developed into a complex internally incoherent monstrosity that could only have been created by a government bureaucracy. . . . it needs at the very least a massive overhaul, and preferably complete termination."

4. Here is a concrete example of how the initial allocation of Freedom Bonds would be determined in the case of a worker who has made Social Security contributions based on average wages during each of the past 35 years. (The average annual wage in 1996 was $25,600.) The amount of Freedom Bonds credited to his account as of January 1, 2000 would be approximately $161,000, determined as follows:

Total employee contributions	$ 36,400
Total employer contributions	$ 36,400
Total contributions	$ 72,800
Less amount used to provide Survivors Insurance and Disability Insurance benefits	$ 19,400
Plus interest on the net contributions	$107,600
Total amount of Freedom Bonds	$161,000

For a worker who has earned the maximum taxable wages for Social Security purposes during each of the past 35 years

($62,700 in 1996), the amount of Freedom Bonds credited to his account as of January 1, 2000 would be approximately $318,000.

5. As of January 1, 2000, the unfunded liability for past-service benefits under the present Social Security system, for persons then less than age 55, is estimated to be about $13 trillion for Old Age, Survivors, and Disability benefits, based on the intermediate-cost assumptions used by the Trustees. The additional liability for Medicare benefits attributable to past service will be even larger, assuming the system is not revised significantly before then.

Chapter 10

1. For a more complete discussion of this question, see: A. Haeworth Robertson, *Social Security: What Every Taxpayer Should Know*, The Retirement Policy Institute, Washington, DC, 1992, Chapter 17.

Index

About the Author

A. Haeworth Robertson was Chief Actuary of the United States Social Security Administration from 1975 to 1978, the period during which attention was first directed toward the significant financial problems that lie ahead. He resigned shortly after the 1977 Amendments to Social Security were passed, believing he could more effectively provide the information necessary to bring about further rational change by working on the "outside."

He has written and lectured widely, giving special emphasis to interpreting and clarifying the financial status of the Social Security program. In 1981 *The Coming Revolution in Social Security,* his first full-length book dealing with Social Security's problems and proposed reforms, was published. In 1992 *Social Security: What Every Taxpayer Should Know* was published. This book was included on the study syllabus for the Society of Actuaries, the Casualty Actuarial Society, and the American Society of Pension Actuaries.

While Chief Actuary of Social Security, he received two awards—the Commissioner's Citation and the Arthur J. Altmeyer Award—for distinguished service in managing the affairs of his office and in explaining Social Security's financial complexities in an easy-to-understand way to the Administration, the Congress, and the public.

Mr. Robertson's actuarial career began in 1953 when, as an officer in the United States Air Force, he served with a special unit of the Department of Defense appointed to prepare an actuarial study of the military retirement system for the 83rd Congress. Since then his entire career has been devoted to personal financial security programs of one kind or another. In addition to serving as Chief Actuary of Social Security, he worked twenty-five years as a consulting actuary dealing with private and public pension plans; five years in organizing, operating, and serving as president of a life insurance company; and ten years as an international consultant on social insurance programs, which involved assignments in Switzerland, Barbados, St. Kitts, Ghana, Lebanon, Kuwait, Turkey, China, Zimbabwe, and the Philippines.

Mr. Robertson received his undergraduate degree in mathematics from the University of Oklahoma in 1951, where he was a Phi Beta Kappa, and his graduate degree in actuarial science from the University of Michigan in 1953. He is a Fellow of the Society of Actuaries, a Fellow of the Conference of Actuaries in Public Practice, a Member of the American Academy of Actuaries, an Associate of the United Kingdom's Institute of Actuaries, and a member of the International Actuarial Association and the International Association of Consulting Actuaries.

Mr. Robertson has served as a member of the Board of Governors and as a Vice President of the Society of Actuaries, and as a member of numerous committees and advisory groups dealing with social insurance and private and public employee pension plans. In 1984 he was selected for a ten-year term and named first chairman of the Department of Defense Retirement Board of Actuaries, a three-person board appointed by the President to oversee the financial operation of the United States military retirement system and report thereon to the President and Congress—a fitting appointment as this is the same retirement system with which he began his actuarial career in 1953.

Mr. Robertson currently resides in the Washington, DC, area, where he is President and Founder of The Retirement Policy Institute, Inc., a Washington-based nonprofit research and education organization devoted to the study of national retirement policy issues. He is listed in *Who's Who in America* and *Who's Who in the World.*

Colophon

This book was set on an Apple Macintosh using QuarkXPress 3.32. Body text is 12 point ITC New Baskerville. Chapter titles and subheads are ITC Franklin Gothic Heavy. The size of the text page is 23 picas by 38 picas. The text paper is 70 pound Springhill Offset.

To Help Increase Understanding of Social Security

The Big Lie: What Every Baby Boomer Should Know About Social Security and Medicare is for everyone concerned about the role that Social Security will play in their own future financial security, as well as the financial security of the nation.

If this book has given you facts and perspectives that help you understand Social Security better and thus enables you to take a more informed position in the ongoing public debate about the future of the system, perhaps you would consider giving copies to your friends and neighbors. People tend to pay more attention to a book if someone they know recommends it or gives it to them. One thing seems certain: more widespread understanding of Social Security is essential if we are to develop a system that is considered to be fair and reasonable by the majority of our citizens.

Please send me additional copies of *The Big Lie: What Every Baby Boomer Should Know About Social Security and Medicare*. I understand I may return books within 15 days for a full refund if not satisfied.

Send me _____ **hardcover copies at $24.95** $_____

Shipping U.S.-Book rate: $3.00 for the first and $2.00 for each additional book. (Surface shipping may take 3-4 weeks.) Priority Mail: $4.00 per book. $_____

5.75% Sales Tax (for orders shipped to Washington, DC and Ohio addresses) $_____

Total $_____

❑ Check enclosed   ❑ Visa   ❑ MasterCard
❑ AMEX   ❑ Discover

Card#_____ Exp.Date _____

Signature _____

Name _____

Address _____

_____

City _____ State _____ Zip _____

FAX orders: (419) 281-6883
Telephone orders: Call Toll Free: 1 (800) 247-6553
Have your AMEX, Discover, VISA or MasterCard ready.
e-mail orders: order@bookmaster.com
Internet orders: http://www.bookmasters.com
Postal orders: BookMasters, Inc., P.O. Box 388, Ashland, OH 44805

To Help Increase Understanding of Social Security

The Big Lie: What Every Baby Boomer Should Know About Social Security and Medicare is for everyone concerned about the role that Social Security will play in their own future financial security, as well as the financial security of the nation.

If this book has given you facts and perspectives that help you understand Social Security better and thus enables you to take a more informed position in the ongoing public debate about the future of the system, perhaps you would consider giving copies to your friends and neighbors. People tend to pay more attention to a book if someone they know recommends it or gives it to them. One thing seems certain: more widespread understanding of Social Security is essential if we are to develop a system that is considered to be fair and reasonable by the majority of our citizens.

Please send me additional copies of *The Big Lie: What Every Baby Boomer Should Know About Social Security and Medicare.* I understand I may return books within 15 days for a full refund if not satisfied.

Send me _____ **hardcover copies at $24.95**	$_____
Shipping U.S.-Book rate: $3.00 for the first and $2.00 for each additional book. (Surface shipping may take 3-4 weeks.) Priority Mail: $4.00 per book.	$_____
5.75% Sales Tax (for orders shipped to Washington, DC and Ohio addresses)	$_____
Total	$_____

❑ Check enclosed ❑ Visa ❑ MasterCard
❑ AMEX ❑ Discover

Card#_____ Exp.Date _____

Signature _____

Name _____

Address _____

_____

City _____ State _____ Zip _____

FAX orders: (419) 281-6883
Telephone orders: Call Toll Free: 1 (800) 247-6553
Have your AMEX, Discover, VISA or MasterCard ready.
e-mail orders: order@bookmaster.com
Internet orders: http://www.bookmasters.com
Postal orders: BookMasters, Inc., P.O. Box 388, Ashland, OH 44805

To Help Increase Understanding of Social Security

The Big Lie: What Every Baby Boomer Should Know About Social Security and Medicare is for everyone concerned about the role that Social Security will play in their own future financial security, as well as the financial security of the nation.

If this book has given you facts and perspectives that help you understand Social Security better and thus enables you to take a more informed position in the ongoing public debate about the future of the system, perhaps you would consider giving copies to your friends and neighbors. People tend to pay more attention to a book if someone they know recommends it or gives it to them. One thing seems certain: more widespread understanding of Social Security is essential if we are to develop a system that is considered to be fair and reasonable by the majority of our citizens.

Please send me additional copies of *The Big Lie: What Every Baby Boomer Should Know About Social Security and Medicare.* I understand I may return books within 15 days for a full refund if not satisfied.

Send me _____ **hardcover copies at $24.95** $_____

Shipping U.S.-Book rate: $3.00 for the first and $2.00 for each additional book. (Surface shipping may take 3-4 weeks.) Priority Mail: $4.00 per book. $_____

5.75% Sales Tax (for orders shipped to Washington, DC and Ohio addresses) $_____

Total $_____

❏ Check enclosed   ❏ Visa   ❏ MasterCard
❏ AMEX   ❏ Discover

Card#_____ Exp.Date _____

Signature _____

Name _____

Address _____

_____

City _____ State _____ Zip _____

FAX orders: (419) 281-6883
Telephone orders: Call Toll Free: 1 (800) 247-6553
Have your AMEX, Discover, VISA or MasterCard ready.
e-mail orders: order@bookmaster.com
Internet orders: http://www.bookmasters.com
Postal orders: BookMasters, Inc., P.O. Box 388, Ashland, OH 44805

To Help Increase Understanding of Social Security

The Big Lie: What Every Baby Boomer Should Know About Social Security and Medicare is for everyone concerned about the role that Social Security will play in their own future financial security, as well as the financial security of the nation.

If this book has given you facts and perspectives that help you understand Social Security better and thus enables you to take a more informed position in the ongoing public debate about the future of the system, perhaps you would consider giving copies to your friends and neighbors. People tend to pay more attention to a book if someone they know recommends it or gives it to them. One thing seems certain: more widespread understanding of Social Security is essential if we are to develop a system that is considered to be fair and reasonable by the majority of our citizens.

Please send me additional copies of *The Big Lie: What Every Baby Boomer Should Know About Social Security and Medicare.* I understand I may return books within 15 days for a full refund if not satisfied.

Send me _____ **hardcover copies at $24.95**	$_____
Shipping U.S.-Book rate: $3.00 for the first and $2.00 for each additional book. (Surface shipping may take 3-4 weeks.) Priority Mail: $4.00 per book.	$_____
5.75% Sales Tax (for orders shipped to Washington, DC and Ohio addresses)	$_____
Total	$_____

❑ Check enclosed   ❑ Visa   ❑ MasterCard
❑ AMEX   ❑ Discover

Card#_____ Exp.Date _____

Signature _____

Name _____

Address _____

_____

City _____ State _____ Zip _____

FAX orders: (419) 281-6883
Telephone orders: Call Toll Free: 1 (800) 247-6553
Have your AMEX, Discover, VISA or MasterCard ready.
e-mail orders: order@bookmaster.com
Internet orders: http://www.bookmasters.com
Postal orders: BookMasters, Inc., P.O. Box 388, Ashland, OH 44805